A SUMMONS TO LIFE

An American Enterprise Institute Book

A SUMMONS TO LIFE

Mediating Structures and the Prevention of Youth Crime

Robert L. Woodson

BALLINGER PUBLISHING COMPANY
Cambridge, Massachusetts
A Subsidiary of Harper & Row, Publishers, Inc.

This book was written under the auspices of a project on mediating structures sponsored by the American Enterprise Institute, Washington, D.C., and funded, in part, by the Division of Education Programs of the National Endowment for the Humanities.

International Standard Book Number: 0-88410-826-0

Library of Congress Catalog Card Number: 81-1179

Printed in the United States of America

Library of Congress Cataloging in Publication Data

Woodson, Robert L.
  A summons to life.

  Includes index.
  1. Juvenile delinquency—United States—Prevention. 2. Juvenile justice, Administration of—United States. 3. Youth—Government policy—United States. 4. Family policy—United States. I. Title.

HV9104.W677	364.3'6'0973	81-1179
ISBN 0-88410-826-0		AACR2

DEDICATION

To
Ellen, Robert, Jr., Ralph, and Jamal and all
those within my extended family

CONTENTS

FOREWORD

Robert Woodson's book is one of several publications to emerge from the project "Mediating Structures and Public Policy" of the American Enterprise Institute. The project, partially supported by funds of the National Endowment for the Humanities, ran from 1976 to 1979. Its codirectors were Richard Neuhaus and myself. The purpose of the project was to explore how mediating structures relate to various areas of public policy at the present time and how more productive relations might be envisaged for the future.

The term "mediating structures," although it has a considerable lineage in social and political thought, may at first sound exotic. Actually, it refers to a commonly experienced reality—namely, those institutions that stand between individuals in their private lives and the vast bureaucratic structures of a modern society. Foremost among these institutions are the family, organized religion, voluntary associations, the neighborhood, and ethnic or racial subcultures. The project was intellectually based on both a sociological perception and a political bias. The sociological perception: that these institutions are vital both to individuals and to society as a whole. The political bias: that democracy, at least in its American form, has a great stake in the survival and well-being of these institutions. This political bias, incidentally, cuts across current dividing lines between "right" and "left" positions on the American scene, and people connected with the project came from diverse points on the ideological spectrum.

The focus of the project was on the welfare state as it now exists in this country. This by no means implied hostility to the concept of the welfare state as such or some romantic notion of seeking its dismantlement. Rather, the project set out to investigate how social justice could be enhanced by greater respect on the part of government for those institutions that provide meaning and identity for most people. For this purpose the project was organized in five panels. In addition to Robert Woodson's panel dealing with problems of criminal justice and crime prevention, there were panels on welfare and child services (Nathan Glazer chairing), housing (John Egan), health (Lowell Levin) and education (David Seeley).

Woodson's approach was distinctive in that it started out with one empirical case, then went on to analyze the reasons for success in that case and further to explore comparable cases elsewhere. The focal case was the House of Umoja, an initiative that had originated spontaneously within the black community in Philadelphia and had achieved some remarkable successes in changing the lives of young people long before any outside agencies took cognizance of it. Woodson's focus on concrete social reality gives his book a tight unity—from the description of the House of Umoja to an analysis of its social and psychological features, to a discussion of comparable experiments in other parts of the country, followed by more general discussions of the wider applicability of this model and its ramification for urban policy in general. In consequence, the reader has no problem following the logic of the argument and developing his own reactions to Woodson's reasoning.

There would be no point summarizing Woodson's argument here; it is clearly presented and stands on its own. A few salient features should be mentioned, though; they will particularly appeal to those with a sociological turn of mind. While Woodson has some critical remarks on current criminological theories, his argument sidesteps the whole debate between "hard" and "soft" theorists. I, for one, am not competent to take a position on this debate, but, at the risk of appearing frivolous, I will confess that it has often impressed me as a contest between those who want more cops and those who want more social workers. Woodson's approach appeals to me because he recommends neither category of officially assigned problem-solvers and tackles the question of youth crime from the standpoint of the community, which in the end is the inevitable context of both crime and crime prevention. This approach puts the emphasis on indigenous forces and initiates, which, by their very nature, are nonbureaucratic and nonprofessionalized. It seems to me that this approach deserves a hearing from both sides of the current debate. It makes no claim to be exclusive or to replace all other existing approaches; it is empirical rather than doctrinaire. What further appeals to me (both as a sociologist and as a citizen) is Woodson's emphasis on values. Whatever else the House of Umoja may be, it is a community built around specific values, and Woodson argues persuasively that this has enabled the young men and women to make a new start in their lives. Put differently, I'm convinced that crime is ultimately rooted in a moral crisis and that its eradication or prevention must therefore be a moral enterprise. In this particular case the values in play derive from black consciousness, but the implications of the case are by no means limited to one set of ideas or to the black community.

Woodson's book is a pioneering effort. This makes for its intense interest, even excitement. By the same token, it cannot provide answers to a number of questions raised by its own argument. I will only mention those that concern me most. (1) What are the likely effects of official recognition and funding on programs such as the ones recommended by Woodson? Put differently, will not such programs lose the very qualities that made them successful once they are clutched in the bureaucratic embrace of public agencies? Woodson faces this question squarely; I don't think that he can fully answer it at this point. (2) Which values can produce the recommended results and which social groups are plausible generators for this sort of initiative? After all, it can hardly be public policy to support *any* values as long as those who espouse them can keep youngsters out of jail; one may think here of Jonestown, of the Mafia, or, for that matter, the Ku Klux Klan. It is also not clear that all social contexts are equally amenable to Woodson's approach; the question of middle class youth crime may be cited here. (3) Can this approach work in the absence of charismatic leadership? (4) Does the approach, as dealing with youth crime, have qualities that might make it difficult to correlate with the various broad policies of urban revitalization that Woodson recommends at the conclusion of his book?

Needless to say, to raise these questions is by no means to denigrate the usefulness of Woodson's book. On the contrary, the book demonstrates its usefulness by raising precisely these questions and opening up the prospect of research designed to answer them. The need for further research and experimentation is one of the most pressing implications of the book.

Peter L. Berger
Professor of Sociology
Boston College

PREFACE

Past and current official approaches to the control and prevention of youth crime have failed to deliver on their promises. Few useful policy recommendations have emerged, despite the millions spent on government-sponsored and private research on youthful offenders. The major result has been the "academicization" of the youth crime issue with its attendant demand for increased expenditures. Liberal attempts to change the behavior of troubled youths by parachuting centrally designed social programs into their neighborhoods have not been effective; nor has the conservative approach of increasing the cost of crime stemmed the tide.

The preponderant evidence indicates that "get tough" deterrence and child welfare and mental health strategies are not reaching a significant population of troubled youths. The courts have relied on these approaches to control violent youth crime, mostly after adjudication. Recently, professional youth service bureaus have even resorted to prevention strategies. Yet the incidence of recidivism and the impact of violent crime in inner city communities remain largely unaffected by these programs. Unfortunately, as our ill-conceived strategies fail to produce the desired results, we seem to lose faith in any possible solutions short of all-out warfare against our urban youth.

It is argued here that a more effective approach to problems of juvenile delinquency lies with the most basic institution of human society—the family. The further strategies for addressing youth problems stray from that unit of society, the more we deceive ourselves about solutions and about the true nature of the problems. The family, neighborhood, and community-based organizations are as I shall show, mediating structures that can provide new approaches to public understanding and a new body of knowledge about the recovery of wayward youth, knowledge sure to benefit the total society.

Moreover, inner city neighborhoods, where social and cultural identities are widely shared, have the potential to act as true communities. They are not mere aggregates displayed in statistics on social problems and social disorganization. They are groups of people who may well be able to act together in conscious awareness of shared problems and relationships. Communities are groups that come to be "for themselves," recognizing the commonality of their life chances and adaptive styles and accepting the responsibility to advance the common good. This authentic sense of community can be activated by indigenous leadership, which shows up again and again in communities throughout the country.

For the mediating structures of family, neighborhood, and local organizations to endure and to maximize their potential, they must play a key role in the restoration of the community at large. Their successes have often been limited by forces over which they have little control, such as housing, employment opportunities, economic policies, and revitalization plans. At present such planning is done in isolation from the needs and realities of mediating structures, with the result that positive local initiatives are often undermined and occasionally destroyed, despite the good intentions of the planners.

This book explores why these local institutions work and examines how social and economic planning has been and continues to be carried out in this country. In particular, the book seeks to identify those policy areas that undermine mediating structures. The last chapter consists of specific policy recommendations that provide a framework to make proper use of the underdeveloped human capital in local communities.

To make proper use of these indigenous resources requires, of course, rethinking the way public policy is developed. It is time to move in a different direction—toward a realization that some of the answers to mental health, crime, and other social problems already exist within the neighborhoods themselves and within their indigenous institutions, both formal and informal.

My sincere appreciation goes to William J. Baroody, Sr., for his support in bringing me to the American Enterprise Institute, and to William J. Baroody, Jr., AEI's president, for his continued advancement of the concept of mediating structures and for seeking to ensure that it receives a fair hearing in debates on public policy. Peter Berger's friendship and personal guidance in reviewing and commenting on material have also been invaluable.

I would also like to express my appreciation to Toye Lewis for her consultation in the preparation of this book. Diane Palm and Janie Ward assisted in field studies, and Ruth Ericson offered research assistance. Paul Pryde, John McKnight, Art Naparstek, and Bob Hill came together as an ad hoc advisory committee to review and comment on the policy recommendations in the final chapter.

Many thanks are extended to Brigitte Berger for her honest and thoughtful comments on the many issues explored here, and to Alfred Herbert of the Lower East Side Family Union for his helpful suggestions on child welfare issues. I am indebted to Professor James Oliver of Cheyney State University for his support and guidance early in my career. Appreciation is also extended to Sister Falaka Fattah and her husband David, and to all of the young men of the House of Umoja, for their trust and cooperation in permitting me access to their sanctuary of human renewal and restoration.

Robert L. Woodson

A GANGWAR APOLOGY

when I think
back on all the fights
fought to uphold a street name
that couldn't holdup
death row houses
surrounded by an invisible wall
where victims of not circumstances
but somechances
challenged their routine bored lives—
and death is real freedom . . .

when I think
back on all the years
wasted like garbage
on a ghetto street corner
and the many friends
blown away like trash
by some strange wind
after a thunder storm boomed
and lightning struck . . .

when I think back on all the drunks
and drug addicts
trying desperately to escape
into a tunnel thru a bottle
or digging holes in their arms
seeking a main line dream
while pimps I admired
danced to the rhythm of prostitutes
who sang dollar Bill . . .

when I think
back on the child
me
wanting to be
somebody/somehow
and
see myself now
as a family man
with job and responsibilities
living in a distant modernized ghetto
as new winds blow
and thunder booms
and lightning strikes—

this ol' tree hunk of a man
bends to apologize
for them/who/like I used to be

refuse
to
T H I N K !

Earle C. Phillips   TH17APR78
Inmate at Gradesford Prison in Pennsylvania

A SUMMONS TO LIFE

1 THE CONTROL OF JUVENILE CRIME

A new, remorseless, mutant juvenile
seems to have been born, and there is
no more terrifying figure in America
today.

Time, July 11, 1977

Mass media and professional journals alike are increasingly concerned with youth crime and with the kind of hard-bitten, alienated young criminals abroad in city streets today. Journalists, social workers, and criminologists report a new breed of young delinquents, preying without mercy on rich and poor alike, on young and old, on neighbors as well as strangers, and acting as often for kicks as for profit.

Public and professional concern about the "new" criminal has in turn reactivated old debates about the causes, the costs, and the appropriate policy for response to juvenile crime. One school of thought still contends that a tougher policy toward violent youths will deter crime. Concurrently, there is a call for lowering the jurisdictional age limit, thus bringing youths accused of serious offenses into the adult system where, if convicted, they could be given a more severe sentence in an adult institution.[1]

Sociologists and psychologists, who note the interrelations of

1

social environment, behavior, and personality, call for policy that addresses the root causes of delinquency. They argue for improving social and economic conditions within the home environment, thought to be productive of delinquency, and for removing the delinquent to noncriminogenic environments and associations. Still another school of thought, and one with considerable influence in criminology, takes the delinquent himself as the principal focus of concern. The objective in this case is to "save the child" through various strategies of mental health, such as psychotherapy or counseling. Justice Department policy officially endorses this child-saving objective.

But a growing number of research studies challenge the general efficacy of these crime control strategies. Of course, any one study is by itself inconclusive and insufficient to rule out any single approach or the theory on which it is based; yet each report on the uncertain or inconsequential effect of a juvenile program adds to the impression that whatever is being done is not enough. The public and the media continue to press for solutions to juvenile crime, but the solutions themselves must apparently include something other than what official juvenile control programs are now doing.

The need to reach youngsters charged with predatory crimes appears especially urgent given the current direction of federal policy toward juvenile offenders. Programs funded through the Office of Juvenile Justice and Delinquency Prevention (OJJDP) under the Department of Justice are highly selective. They are consciously oriented toward nonchronic offenders, status offenders (that is, those whose offenses would not be offenses if committed by an adult), and those charged with less serious infractions of the law.

OJJDP, which is officially committed to reforming offenders and to more efficient delivery of its battery of services to youths in trouble, openly acknowledges that some hard-core offenders remain resistant to any approach now offered. Hard-core or high-risk offenders are defined as those unreachable through counseling, job programs, halfway homes, retraining, or other forms of professional supervision. For them, incarceration is still recommended as the appropriate institutional response in the absence of workable alternatives.

Thus, the OJJDP is caught between apparently conflicting objectives as it fulfills its functions. Public concern for the safety of the streets and the costs of crime must be balanced against public demand for the rehabilitation of young offenders. (We must "save the child.") Rehabilitation suggests the need for programs that change the individual offender as a means of controlling crime. Yet the record shows that such approaches to juveniles are apparently reserved for low-risk offenders,[2] while those who present the highest risk and therefore concern the public most are untreated, jailed, retained for a short period, and returned to the streets unchanged—and probably even more embittered.

There is no lack of professional comment on this situation. Testifying before the Senate subcommittee on juvenile delinquency in April 1978, Michael E. Smith, director of the Vera Institute, stated, "As we approach the day when the 'virgins and boy scouts' have been leveraged out of incarceration into community-based treatment programs, we may be left with a small but very visible institutional population of chronic offenders for whom there are no realistic and well-designed community-based treatment alternatives."[3]

An even more important point is that as the Office of Juvenile Justice "saves children" and "protects the public" by factoring the delinquent population into "amenable" and "resistant" categories, researchers call attention to the social composition of the two groups created and to the predictable consequences of this differential application of juvenile justice. Frank Zimring in a recent report for the Twentieth Century Fund observes:

- Males between the ages of 13 and 20 comprise nine percent of the [delinquent] population, but account for more than half of all property crime arrests and more than a third of all offenses involving violence.
- Violent crime by the young has increased.
- Most young offenders who commit acts of extreme violence and pursue criminal careers come from *minority, ghetto and poverty* backgrounds; so do their victims. [Emphasis added.][4]

Zimring predicted in an earlier study commissioned by OJJDP that youth crime rates would slowly abate over the next decade because of the decline in birthrates in the general population. But, significantly, he found that birthrates for minorities will not decrease substantially. In fact, young urban black males between the ages of eighteen and twenty will increase 8 percent over the next fifteen to twenty years.[5]

The implications are clear. A series of trends is converging, and OJJDP programs are seen to be segregating the nation's delinquent youth by race and class. Even as overall rates of delinquency abate, the delinquent group will include a growing proportion of poor and minority children.

Moreover, since most diversion and prevention initiatives are carried out by nonprofit organizations that typically do not serve the urban minorities,[6] the children being "saved" in treatment programs will continue to be white middle-class youngsters, with everyone else remanded to custodial care. The OJJDP failure to provide effective rehabilitation for the poor, urban, minority youths who increasingly make up their clientele in turn reinforces a policy direction toward the imposition of harsher treatment of juveniles, including lowering the jurisdictional age to make youths accessible to heavier judgments of the adult court.

The segregation of delinquent youths into two categories—those amenable and those resistant to treatment—follows racial and class lines and relates to theories of appropriate institutional response to delinquency. Put bluntly, a "get tough" policy is discovered to be appropriate for chronic, resistant youth, while some form of "saving" seems especially suitable for low-risk, tractable offenders.

In this context "high risk" means those youths who show the least probability of changing and reforming as a result of rehabilitation treatment. When such youths are included in various treatment services they disproportionately lower the success rate of the program as measured by the extent of subsequent recidivism. Conversely, when high-risk types can be identified and excluded from programs, the measured effectiveness of treatment is found to be stronger. Rehabilitation succeeds best, in other words, with the youth who is less involved in crime and whose crimes are less serious. High-risk clients have committed more serious offenses and are repeaters, urban, poor, and members of a minority. This group, more visible than ever, appears as the "new" predatory criminals of media fame and popular concern. Moreover, according to demographic reports, the social category from which this group is drawn will probably increase if present trends continue.

By the 1990s a majority of black youths, particularly black males, will have been in trouble with the law, and a serious proportion of this group will have been involved in violent crimes. Yet there is strong evidence that federal agencies such as OJJDP have virtually written off this group. Urban minority males, who, it is predicted, will commit a great deal of the most costly crimes, are precisely those Americans least well provided for in institutional policy and social services.

To honor both our commitment to rehabilitate offenders and our concern for public safety, we must reconsider our approach to the entire juvenile delinquent population and especially the minority, urban delinquents for whom current programs are apparently inappropriate and who as a group will increasingly commit the crimes we fear. To save the next generation of minority men and the families for which they will be responsible, we must discover programs that are effective and deploy funds accordingly.

To clarify the criticism of current policy and practice, I shall first review some basic assumptions of the policies and programs of the Office of Juvenile Justice. I shall argue that the insufficiencies and outright failures of these approaches can be traced in part to ideologies and in part to structural factors. Some unofficial, but more successful, control programs that have appeared in many urban centers will then be discussed.

FACTS OF JUVENILE JUSTICE POLICY

Professionals in the field generally concede that a wide variety of resources are needed to handle different kinds of young offenders and potential offenders if we are to improve the performance of the juvenile justice system and uphold the ideological commitment to justice. But research continues to show that the methods used to deal with delinquency are generally of doubtful or insignificant effect, especially for high-risk or hard-core delinquents. A disturbing proportion of the clients of the system are neither deterred nor rehabilitated by what is done for them. In fact, there is reason to think that in some cases the intervention may even be counterproductive. Significantly, President Johnson's Commission on Law Enforcement (President's Commission, 1967) recommended that the best service for a potential client of the juvenile justice system would be to divert him or her from it.

Although a comprehensive review of research in the field cannot be attempted here, a brief summary of some key studies will underline the issues and performance problems faced by the juvenile correction system. I shall summarize some of the research that has been done and indicate the conclusions drawn from that research by many of the concerned professionals.

What The Research Shows

There has been a definite shift in official policy away from purely retributive or punitive approaches in handling of juveniles. Instead of dealing simply with past misdeeds, officials have tried to deter potential delinquency and to prevent recidivism through treatment programs that attempt to alter the variables thought to be associated with delinquency. Much that is written frames the juvenile justice system in an ideology of concern for the delinquent himself—"saving the child." The system wants to do well, but it also wants to do good.

One consequence of this orientation is increased interest in empirical research into the effectiveness of punishments and of available alternatives. Much of this research has consisted of matching rates of recidivism with categories of offenses, with social characteristics of offenders, and with the treatment or correction applied to the offender. Efforts have also been made before and after treatment to study changes in attitudes, values, and other personality variables linked with deviance. The methodological problems of this research, however, are constantly being emphasized by researchers themselves. It seems that in spite of the obvious need for correctional administrators to have reliable information about the effect of various approaches, virtually nothing is known about the extent to which deterrence is achieved. Rehabilitation or positive change in the young offender as a result of treatment appears to be dubious or uneven.

Research results are inconclusive or generally discouraging for all types of treatment. Tests of attitude change, for example, can distinguish reliably between delinquents and nondelinquents, but cannot distinguish clearly between various treatments in terms of outcome.[7] Probation seems to be at least as effective as institutional sentencing, especially for first offenders;[8] yet no research shows that probation is especially effective in deterring the offender from future involvement with the courts.[9] Fines and discharges are more effective than probation or imprisonment for first offenders and recidivists of all ages, yet not especially effective and not evenly or predictably effective for all categories of offenders. In other research longer institutional sentences are found to be no more effective in preventing recidivism than shorter ones.[10]

On the question of increasing the success rates of programs by allocating treatment according to the type of offender, research once again offers little firm evidence on which to base administrative or policy decisions. The offenders most likely to improve, regardless of the type of treatment, are the so-called medium risks;[11] yet no typology of offenders or treatments has been shown to be either valid or reliable, and no relations have been conclusively established between any type of treatment and any type of offender.[12]

Other research into the effectiveness of various institutional responses and treatments is similarly discouraging. Many studies reveal no significant differences, as measured by rates of reconviction, among the types of treatment investigated. Where overall differences in reconviction rates between treatment and control groups are discovered, serious methodological shortcomings are alleged. In a review of 100 evaluative studies of this kind, W.C. Bailey found a successful outcome reported in about half the studies, but the more rigorous the research design, the higher the percentage reporting no change. Evidence supporting the efficacy of the treatments reviewed is "slight, inconsistent and of questionable reliability," remarks Bailey.[13]

Robert Martinson, in a detailed evaluation of 231 recidivism studies made between 1945 and 1967, reached similar conclusions. He asserts that no sure way has been found to reduce recidivism through rehabilitation: "We haven't the faintest clue." Martinson examined a range of treatment techniques, including education, vocational training, individual counseling, group counseling, transformation of the institutional environment, and medical treatment. "Nothing works," he concluded.[14] Martinson and others have also noted the general inability to translate assumptions behind correctional practice into meaningful policy.[15] The relation between theory and what is in fact experienced by those being treated is uncertain, to say the least. The point here, of course, is not to criticize the status of research on these questions, but rather to underscore the practical problem of designing programs that will actually help young offenders and potential offenders.

Jerome Miller points out still another uncomfortable fact about the juvenile justice programs. Calling the corrections bureaucracies a "system of keepers and captives," he argues that the development of diagnostic categories—ostensibly for a better match between individuals and programs to increase the effectiveness of treatment—results in defining the failures as outside the expertise and responsibility of the helping profession.[16]

> The sad truth is that, despite rhetoric, we have had an inverse system whereby those most likely to present major problems to society in terms of violence or repeated crimes are systematically excluded from the system of care by professional diagnosis and are thereby relegated to the largest, most impersonal human warehouses—jails, prisons, training schools—where they find the fewest and least qualified professional "helpers."[17]

We thus effectively exonerate the professional staffs through the manipulation of assigned categories, while placing blame for rehabilitation failure "squarely on the failures themselves."

Not surprisingly, perhaps, the young offenders who are designated failures of the rehabilitation ethic and are "warehoused" at the deep end of the correctional system turn out to be the less educated, nonwhite delinquents of low socioeconomic status.[18] Yet it is precisely this category of excluded minority youth for whom society most needs to devise effective means of deterrence and rehabilitation, according to many observers. As research shows, the social urgency of improving our services to minority youths of low socioeconomic status is apparent in the increased rate and seriousness of the social harm for which young people in this category are as a group responsible.

The point is clearly brought out in a report by Marvin Wolfgang[19] in which data were derived from a time analysis tracing delinquency of a birth cohort of Philadelphia youths. For the entire cohort 35 percent were delinquent, having at least one contact with the police; slightly more than half (50.24 percent) of the Negro boys in the cohort were delinquent. Significantly, the category of nonwhite delinquents of low socioeconomic status had the lowest IQ, the lowest achievement level in school, made the most residential and school moves (measures associated with delinquency), and least frequently completed twelfth grade. Nonwhites had an offense rate three times higher than whites.

Analysis further shows that nearly three-fourths of the offenses committed by one-time offenders were petty, often juvenile status offenses, such as truancy, running away, or "incorrigibility." In general only about 30 percent of the cohort's offenses were index crimes as defined in the Uniform Crime Reports system—acts of injury, theft, or damage.

Slightly more than half (55 percent) of all offenders were recidivists. Chronic offenders or heavy repeaters, who committed five or more offenses while of juvenile court age, constitute only 6.3 percent of the birth cohort and 18 percent of the delinquent subset. Yet these 627 boys were responsible for 5,305 delinquencies, or 52 percent of all delinquencies committed by the entire birth cohort.

In addition, chronic offenders are heavily represented among those who commit the index offenses. Of the 815 personal attacks (rape, homicide, aggravated assault, and simple assault), 53 percent were committed by chronic offenders. Of the 2,257 property offenses, 62 percent were by chronics. Of the 193 robberies, 71 percent were by chronics. Of all violent offenses committed by nonwhites, 70 percent were by chronic offenders, compared with 45 percent by chronic offenders who were white. These nonwhite chronic offenders represent the hard-core delinquents who are being warehoused, rather than treated for rehabilitation. Wolfgang insists, "That such a high proportion of offenses—particularly serious acts of violence—are committed by a relatively small number of offenders—is a fact that loudly claims attention for a social policy of intervention with the 'hard core' group."[20]

The report also shows that nonwhites have higher rates than whites for all three categories of violent offenses combined: Nonwhites have six times the rate of whites for assault offenses, four times the rate of whites for property offenses, and twenty times the rate of whites for robberies.

Wolfgang claims that important policy implications can be drawn from this comparison of rates of serious crime for different categories of offenders and offenses. His first suggestion is that the most efficient time for social intervention seems to be when someone has committed his first offense. To deter the child at this point would have the greatest effect, he says, reducing the number of all offenses, but more significantly affecting the incidence of index offenses, which draw the most concern in deterrence and prevention programs.

Since more nonwhites are repeat offenders and account for more of the index offenses, the second policy implication Wolfgang suggests would be that this social group be made the object of major efforts. Instead of systematically isolating these youths from the more sophisticated deterrence and rehabilitation programs, we must concentrate our resources on nonwhites of low socioeconomic status (SES), the group from which are drawn a disproportionate number of violent chronic delinquents: "The sheer size of offenses of bodily harm committed by nonwhite lower SES boys who are recidivists is alone a measure of their importance for promoting some kinds of intervention as a basis of prevention. . . ."[21] Wolfgang, a leading criminologist, claims that more social harm is created by nonwhites, so that resources of treatment and harm reduction should be mostly employed among nonwhite youths. By focusing resources and attention on the lower socioeconomic status nonwhite subset of a birth cohort who have a first delinquency, not only would the general rate of delinquency be affected, but also the most serious acts involving physical assault or violence on others would be drastically decreased.[22]

Research in crime and delinquency also attempts to account for the apparent association between race, high rates of crime, and urban living. There are no doubt good reasons for skepticism about any criminal statistics that report the race of the offender (blacks appear to suffer more injustices than whites in the law enforcement process from the time of arrest to imprisonment), but even the most valid efforts to measure crime place black crime rates high. Moreover, black populations have come to be highly concentrated in inner city ghettos, so that concern with crime in the city necessarily directs attention to this group. Research has tried to show how much variance in the crime statistics is accounted for by the different characteristics of the category of youths juvenile justice bureaucracies have identified as high-risk: low socioeconomic status, minority culture, and urban background. The question is: What is the interaction among these factors, and how are they associated with delinquency?

Research makes it clear that urban living, not race itself, is the critical factor contributing to the initiation of delinquency. Any group that has to live with the same perverse and unfavorable inner city circumstances as they will come to exhibit the same high crime rates associated with urban blacks. In addition, experts suspect a link between three conditions—physical features of parts of a city, certain social-psychological patterns, and a tradition of lawlessness. No one can yet show that these three conditions are invariable or even highly probable consequences of urban life, but the research community continues to assume strong links in the absence of a successful demonstration to the contrary.

The reasoning and facts behind the assumption are these: Urban living is much more anonymous than nonurban, usually permitting more freedom from the constraints common in tradition-oriented communities and sometimes in rural areas, and providing greater freedom to deviate. Control is impersonalized in the city. It is directed by distant bureaucracies and executed by police and other authorities who are strangers to the people they control. Anonymity in city living is apt to be associated with a lessening of motivation to obey external demands, and there are fewer interpersonal or internalized inhibitions against deviance. The close presence of more people and their possessions and the continuous close display of desirable, portable consumer goods create greater opportunity for theft. Since victims are anonymous, acts against them are impersonal. Poverty and blocked opportunity are apt to be accompanied by frustration, internalized cultural strains between the means available and the ends desired, conflicting norms, and anomie. All are probably, if not invariably, linked with urban living conditions and a street tradition of delinquent and criminal behavior.

Population density, spacial mobility, ethnic and class heterogeneity, reduced family functions, and greater anonymity—all characterize urban more than nonurban life. When found in high degree and when combined with a certain litany of sociological ills, these traits are generally assumed to be criminogenic, fostering the social-psychological mechanisms just mentioned from which deviance is most likely to emerge. Other urban features such as poverty, physical deterioration, little education, residence in industrial and commercial centers, unemployment or unskilled labor, economic dependency, marital instability, overcrowding, lack of legitimate opportunities to make a better life, the absence of positive anticriminal behavior patterns, higher frequency of organic diseases, and cultural inferiority are all strongly associated with the chance of delinquency.[23] These features also describe the living conditions and the social psychology to which minority children are as a group especially exposed. To deal with nonwhite delinquent youth is to take into account at some level the complex of factors here sketched; it is to deal with the physical deterioration and overcrowding that beset inner city populations, with the psychological effects of anonymity and blocked opportunity, and with the "culture of poverty" in which a tradition of law-lessness feeds on deprivation and despair.

Summary and Discussion

When the research on issues and problems in the field of juvenile corrections is reviewed, the foregoing facts stand out. In the last ten or fifteen years, official policy has shifted away from a purely retributive-punitive approach in corrections and toward efforts to deter potential delinquency and to prevent recidivism through treatment and resocialization. As a result of this policy change, special programs, grounded in theoretical social science, have been set up to provide "innovative alternatives" to human warehousing. Although put forth as liberal alternatives to punishment and coercive control, these programs generally turn out to have the same dubious and unclear relation to the achievement of their objectives as did deterrence through punishment and threat of punishment. The effectiveness of the alternative approaches is so unclear it hardly justifies the professional input.

Moreover, the most elaborate care and treatment in professionally designed programs seem to be assigned to youths who predictably are at least risk of possible future delinquency, are least apt to be involved with serious index offenses, and are most likely to reform no matter what is done to or for them. Whatever success alternative programs have seems due at least in part to the expedient of factoring out the most risky and most resentful delinquents, who are consistently urban, nonwhite, and of low socioeconomic status. The picture is one of generally poor or uncertain performance of rehabilitation programs, as well as selective response to the delinquent population to be served. Miller shows that these urban blacks, potentially embarrassing to the liberal aims of the juvenile justice system, are in one way or another relabeled as "undeserving" of or "not amenable" to new treatment modalities.[24] They are, as "outsiders," still remanded to the theoretically discredited custodial and detention centers, where they are left untreated, retained, and released basically without benefit of professional effort to help them.

Miller calls these lower class, nonwhite delinquents "strangers" in the juvenile justice system. Of all those brought before the courts, these strangers least resemble the bureaucratic staff that judges and retains them, and they are most apt to reappear in court and for the worst offenses. Poor, black, undereducated, urban youth are stigmatized by a "spoiled" social identity that bedevils their chances before they ever encounter juvenile justice and seemingly even when they find themselves within its jurisdiction. Yet they make up a category of offenders by all indications most in need of attention. Successful intervention with these youths promises the biggest reward in terms of protecting society's interests, to say nothing of protecting the interests of the troubled young people themselves.

APPROACHES TO THE CONTROL AND PREVENTION OF YOUTH CRIME

Criminal justice is a pragmatic business. It is concerned with results, with the actual relation between various penal measures and their deterrent effect, usually measured by rates of recidivism. The prime business of the courts and correctional agencies is to maintain the normative order of society by inducing conformity to its rules.

But institutional responses to delinquent and criminal behavior are not merely pragmatic, automatically matching punishment and crime for maximum effect. At every step in the practical pursuit of behavior control, judgments and interpretations are made of the law, of conventions for applying the law, and of the behavior at hand. These judgments are organized according to certain basic assumptions, typical of our culture, that seem to account for the delinquency and to dictate the appropriate strategy for control.

Domination and subordination, authority and obedience, privilege and deference are characteristics of the institutional structure within which justice is meted out and society's rules defended. Noncompliance is typically explained in one of three ways: (1) the subordinate whose behavior is monitored is unaware of the rules; (2) he is "sick" in some sense and cannot comply; or (3) he is simply willful. If he has had insufficient opportunity to learn the rules or has learned the wrong ones, logically we must alter his learning milieux and retrain him. If he is psychologically unable to perform correctly, we must "cure" him. If, on the other hand, he is merely self-willed and obstinate, we must "get tough." In this case, we must raise the cost to him of his delinquency until he succumbs. We punish infractions to promote compliance in something reminiscent of Bentham's "hedonistic calculus."

The possibility that the rules might be somehow wrong or perhaps impossible to follow cannot be considered within the procedures or programs spawned by correctional policy. Only facts of noncompliance and assumptions about the condition of the delinquent are taken into account in framing strategies of institutional response. These strategies are beset with a variety of problems, but they share three serious limitations: (1) the focus of each strategy is narrow; (2) the youths themselves are allowed little or nothing to say about the design and operation of the programs constructed to control them; and (3) the involuntary participation of the youths is often pathogenic, with few, if any, redeeming qualities. In all cases, problem-solving methods have been conceived and controlled by professionals external to the population at risk. The following sections examine the three basic assumptions about delinquent behavior and the associated control strategy and raise questions about certain implications and derivative facts of these three approaches.

Get Tough with Young Criminals

The "get tough" policy is taken to be an appropriate response to the willful malefactor. (Some see all delinquency as mere willful disobedience.) "Get tough" implies a preference for incarceration and punishment over treatment. Punishment is as harsh as is thought necessary to deter the child from repeating his offenses. There is no precise calculus of the degree of harshness effective for deterrence of different types of offenders and offenses, but the theory that harshness is a deterrent to delinquency continues to be popular.

Perhaps in part because professional programs of juvenile correction have not achieved convincing results with violent urban youth, some theorists suspect there may be no solution short of open warfare and punitive incarceration. In an associated line of reasoning, more and more public notice is given to theories of genetic failure, which also underwrite "get tough" policies.

Yet anyone familiar with the environment of urban delinquents and gangs must realize that such youths have been subjected to threats and coercion for most of their lives. Threatening them with additional punitive harshness is like threatening a kamikaze pilot with death. For a youth who already copes with armed rival gang members and faces death daily, what inhibiting effect can "tough" policies have?

Each time the press reports the case of a young person brutally beating or robbing an elderly person, there is a public outcry and demands that harsher penalties be given for such offenses and that the jurisdictional age limit be lowered. Some even advocate the continued detention of certain youthful offenders after the completion of their prison terms. Politicians successfully campaign on a "get tough" platform, and within the criminal justice system itself the punitive preference is clearly reflected in policy debates and planning.

It is understandable that retribution is desired by anyone who has been a victim of an assault or whose friend or loved one has suffered injury at the hands of an attacker. Nevertheless, this psychologically understandable desire for retribution must not be allowed to be translated into punitive public policy. In the words of James Wilson, we must not "fund our fears."[25] To do so threatens our democratic constitutional form of government through the potential subversion of basic constitutional guarantees protecting all citizens.

In fact, the evidence of an erosion of constitutional rights is mounting. For example, proponents of the Omnibus Crime Control and Safe Streets Act of 1968 advocated massive financial assistance to local police departments to improve their capacity to prevent and control crime. The act established the Law Enforcement Assistance Administration (LEAA) within the Department of Justice and has since provided millions of federal dollars to strengthen local police departments. Title II of the bill would have allowed confessions to be taken without a lawyer's presence. It would also have allowed for detention of a criminal suspect without prompt arraignment and suspension of the writ of habeas corpus for those previously convicted of a crime. The bill also legitimated wiretapping. Title I would have exempted police departments from compliance with the 1964 Civil Rights Act, which prohibits federal support to any agency engaged in racial discrimination.

Supporters of the bill justified its unconstitutionality by contending that certain measures would be used only against "criminals." George Napper, criminologist and currently chief of police in Atlanta, observed:

> The provision of the bill required us to trust the discretionary powers of the police and to believe that they would not abuse such power. The police

would decide who is and who is not a criminal. The Fifth Amendment, through the due process clauses, acknowledges that the writers of the Constitution did not have such faith and historically the American public have not demonstrated such faith. The frightening implications of having such provisions in a democratic society are apparent and need no elaboration.[26]

Although many of the more restrictive provisions of the bill were finally deleted, some final provisions confirmed the worst fears of its opponents regarding its constitutionality. The wiretap provisions, for instance, remained, and proponents within the Justice Department argued that this measure was needed to combat espionage, homicide, kidnapping, and organized crime. In three years following the passage and implementation of the wiretap provision, however, out of a total of 1,118,912 times used, wiretapping was not employed in a homicide case or in an espionage case and was used only once in a kidnapping case. Instead, it was used primarily against people viewed as political dissidents.[27]

Aside from the danger of erosive effects on our constitutional guarantees, the "get tough" policies have failed measurably to fulfill their promise to reduce crime among target populations of criminals and suspects.[28]

In 1970 under the Nixon administration, the Congress passed a law pertaining to the District of Columbia that allowed the detention of criminal suspects before formal charges were brought against them. (This practice, popularly known as "preventive detention,"[29] is in force as a legal sanction in South Africa and is widely used in communist countries.) The law also made it possible for the police to enter unannounced the premises of persons suspected of trafficking in illegal drugs. This was done to prevent a suspect from destroying evidence. Governor Rockefeller of New York succeeded in getting enacted a measure intended to stop or seriously limit drug trafficking there. The new law provided for a mandatory life sentence for offenders caught with a certain quantity of narcotics. All three measures—preventive detention as a federal policy, "no knock" in Washington, D.C., and the Rockefeller drug law in New York—proved to be poor deterrent measures and invited miscarriages of justice. Currently, these laws are either unused or being considered for repeal, but "get tough" is still endorsed by many and still contends for implementation in justice policies.

The costs of enforcing deterrence strategies are another cause for concern. With the burgeoning taxpayers' revolt, the American public may soon be unwilling to pay such a high price for such poor results. In New York State, where approximately 2,000 juvenile offenders are committed to maximum security detention facilities, the annual cost for the care of each youth ranges from $30,000 to $50,000.[30] The cost of constructing and maintaining a new jail facility is in the millions.

Moreover, jails and detention facilities not only fail to rehabilitate inmates, but often make them worse. In the District of Columbia's juvenile detention facility in 1975, there was one suicide every week for six consecutive weeks. In similar facilities around the country, gang sodomy is an induction ritual. People enter jails as amateur criminals and emerge confirmed in their own criminal identity, having acquired practical information and defensive ideological rationales for the more successful pursuit of a criminal career. Even if jail terms were lengthened, as some now propose, 90 percent of all prisoners would one day return to society. After their release they are more hardened than before incarceration; more, not less, committed to a criminal perspective; and more often than not a menace to themselves, to their families, and to their communities.

It would be wrong to conclude from these comments that deterrent sanctions have no function whatever for limiting criminal behavior. A minority of individuals who defy control by any other means must be separated from the rest of society and confined until some effective alternative is available. But young people who go to prison as punishment should not be subjected to other punishment once they are there, as now happens in youth prisons, where little attention is given to prisoners' human needs.

Alter the Adverse Environment

At the other extreme, some social commentators and welfare professionals maintain that violent and criminal acts among youth can be prevented and controlled only by addressing the complex social and economic problems within the youth's immediate environment. The environment itself is seen as the root cause of the problem. This line of reasoning is the basis for two approaches popular with social welfare bureaucracies. One would remove suspected and convicted persons from their home communities and place them in detention and rehabilitation centers. The other proposes a massive overhaul of urban neighborhoods, job development and training, desegregation of public schools, and even reform of the public welfare system. Crime control is to be the result of breaking the link between the crime-prone individual and the criminogenic environment.

Child welfare systems have placed great emphasis on changing the individual by removing him from poor, questionable home environments and retraining him in artificial remedial environments. New evidence, however, indicates that these alternatives to home environments are not helpful to the children, but in fact many children begin delinquent careers because of the child welfare system.

In May 1977 the Office of the Comptroller, Bureau of Municipal Investigation and Statistics of the City of New York, conducted an audit of the private, voluntary, nonprofit foster care agencies serving the city's dependent and neglected children.[31] The findings illustrate both the horrors of institutionalizing young people and the costly futility of this approach to controlling delinquent behavior.

In New York approximately 29,000 children in individual family foster care entail an overall annual cost of $280 million, or $10,000 per child. The majority of the children are cared for by thirty-five voluntary agencies funded almost completely by the city, state, and federal governments. Over half the money goes for administrative overhead and social services. Many of these agencies depend entirely on tax dollars for their survival. The auditors found that of 35,657 children in all types of foster care (including group homes) during 1976, only 5,431 were discharged to permanent homes. The number being released each year nearly equaled the number entering care. The effect of this low discharge rate is that 11,000 children remain in care, on the average of 5.5 percent per year, more than necessary, at a cost of $233 million to the taxpayer. Many of these children spend the rest of their lives in care. Twenty-nine percent of the children sampled have been in three or more foster homes, with debilitating effect.

When a parent has abandoned a child or the child is severely abused or neglected or mentally incapacitated, the agency is expected to seek the release of the child for adoption. In 110 cases reviewed by the city auditors, only eight were released in good time and only twenty-two others after many years of care. New York State law requires that children eligible for adoption be photo listed with the state adoption service, but since only 24 percent of the available children were in fact listed, many children were not known to prospective adoptive parents.

The foster care agencies claim that many children are in foster care because of the lack of prospective parents, particularly for so-called hard-to-place (largely minority and older) children. A poll of prospective parents inquiring about adoption, however, indicated that the agencies' policies and attitudes had discouraged them. In addition, 30 percent of the parents wanted minority children, and one parent in ten wanted a child eight years or older.

These facts raise serious questions about crime prevention policies that feature removing the child from his home. Furthermore, of the children identified as juvenile delinquents in New York City in a given year, one-third have been in foster care. On the record, this number corresponds with the percentage that shows signs of psychological and emotional instability brought on by moving from one foster home to another. These dependent and neglected children are, for the most part (82 percent), voluntarily placed in the child care system by their natural parents, who expect that their children will receive better care than they can give. In fact, in return for this confidence they experience betrayal.[32]

Since year in and year out institutionalization does not rehabilitate the thousands of youths so treated, the continued appeal by social workers for the maintenance of institutions is open to question. Some critics of the child welfare system suggest that many are being maintained strictly for the revenues they produce for staff. It is suggested that extrinsic reasons, rather than any valuable rehabilitation effects on incarcerated youth, account for the continued appeal by welfare professionals for the maintenance of institutions.[33]

The second way to separate youth from dangerous environments calls for reconstructing the urban neighborhood itself and reorganizing its institutional structure. Price tags for these efforts range in the billions of dollars at a time when the American economy is in trouble and the average taxpayer, feeling the economic squeeze, is unwilling to support such costly change.

Many community organization efforts in the 1960s, funded by the Office of Economic Opportunity and inspired by the President's Commission on the Prevention of Juvenile Delinquency, aimed at preventing delinquency by removing social, educational, and economic barriers to achievement among youths. Programs such as the national job corps, neighborhood youth corps, domestic peace corps (ACTION), and local youth development projects such as HARYOU-ACT emphasized education and job training for inner city youth. Programs such as HARYOU-ACT and Mobilization for Youth in New York City also engaged in community organization to improve the coordination and utilization of traditional social services. These efforts were known as social change strategies.

During the early Mobilization for Youth planning, research sociologists often advised that community solidarity is essential to delinquency prevention, but they were not taken seriously by the cadres of Great Society bureaucrats who emerged in the mid- to late 1960s. Richard Cloward, Lloyd Ohlin, and others were attempting to illustrate through their programs that social control could be more meaningful and effective when developed within the community in question, with maximum involvement of the youngsters themselves in decisions about the programs.

The systems change theories, while espousing the need for the mobilization of community residents and for their active involvement in social change, resulted in political battles between Washington officials and local politicians over policies and money, competition among the professional social work groups over control of the programs, and only selective cooperation of the indigenous leadership. It was soon apparent that instead of federal grants going to support community-based groups and institutions, funds were directed to the traditional social service agencies, all with headquarters and policy making outside the target areas.

Kenneth Clark, a leading spokesman for the Harlem community, led a protest against these developments. He characterized the power plays between politicians and social workers over control of ghetto reform as "social work colonialism."[34] Clark's description of the problem was controversial but accurate, since community residents were given no real decision-making power and were responsible for training youth for nonexistent jobs. Efforts were directed toward establishing idealized democratic institutions, with little consideration of the genuine needs of local people or real involvement of the youths and their families. Instead, middle-class–oriented social work practices were imposed on poverty-ridden communities.

The major shortcoming of these programs lay in the narrowly focused strategies, which suggested that delinquent behavior could be changed merely by providing short-term training and a low-wage job. Lerone Bennett, noted black historian, remarked in assessing these programs, "Our children need inspiration, motivation and direction as much as they need jobs."[35]

The Mental Health Approach

Another approach, somewhere between tough deterrence and environmental change, maintains that delinquency can be prevented and controlled by altering the behavior of youths directly through various techniques of mental health, such as psychotherapy or counseling. In fact, mental health intervention has received almost as much professional attention and funding as the deterrence approach.

A broad cross section of American society relies heavily on the psychiatric-psychotherapeutic complex to provide answers to a host of interpersonal and intragroup problems. The criminal justice system, in particular, places great credence on the theories and opinions of mental health professionals in a wide variety of situations, including:

- Determining the mental competence of an accused person to stand trial
- Making psychiatric treatment a condition of diversion from the criminal justic system
- Diagnostically screening both before and after sentencing
- Negotiating the release of hostages seized in the commission of a felony

In addition, mental health professionals may be called upon by law enforcement agencies and the news media to provide a descriptive personality profile of persons who are wanted for heinous crimes, as was done in the case of David Berkowitz ("Son of Sam") in New York City.

The mental health methods are firmly entrenched throughout the spectrum of justice services. Professional diagnoses, coupled with interpretation of data using computer extrapolations, complete the impression that only the trained professional has knowledge of the dynamics of human interaction. Burton J. Bledstein made a similar point in his book, *The Culture of Professionalism.*[36] He noted that the conditions of modern society place a high premium on esoteric knowledge, especially when it comes stamped with the special authority of an organized community of practitioners who police each other's opinions and thereby create standards of competence.

The personnel of the mental health establishment are upper middle class, which is reflected in the norms, procedures, and cultural climate of therapeutic practice. Although traditional mental health practices may be useful in addressing problems among people who share the same or similar cultural values, they have made only limited inroads in providing effective service to clients of the criminal justice system, who are for the most part poor and young members of minority ethnic groups.[37]

Another feature of mental health practice that limits its ability to serve poor and minority communities is the emphasis on a disease-pathology model of deviance. Lower class client communities are looked upon as a kaleidoscope of interlocking pathologies. Not surprisingly, mental health approaches have been seen as especially appropriate for the rehabilitation of lower class delinquents.

With marginal variations in emphasis and ideology, the juvenile justice bureaucracy has presented over the past ten to fifteen years two major models for the mental health approach to juvenile offenders. The first model has a psychiatric orientation and was conceived as a therapeutic alternative to purely retributive or punitive approaches. The second has been brought forward as an innovative alternative and is oriented to small group theory. In one form or another, both models are still being funded, staffed, and studied for effectiveness. Clear confirmation of effectiveness, however, is still lacking.

Model I   Once it has been determined that the individual youth is in need of correction, he or she is placed in a psychology-based youth correctional facility where appropriate control over his or her thinking and behavior can be maintained. Programs of athletics, academic education, and vocational training may be offered there as healthy activities for an adolescent; these are not only substantively worthwhile but also effective since through such activities he or she will encounter appropriate values and participate in rule-governed social interaction. A system of rewards and penalties is usually set up, consisting of badges, prizes, or privileges given or withheld according to the individual's conformity to the control system of the institution.

Because the individual is thought to be "sick" as a result of faulty personality formation, his treatment is deliberately framed as a resocialization program, with strategies to facilitate appropriate role modeling. Social relations between members of the therapeutic staff and the child are structured as an authoritarian association of unequals in which reidentification and curative transference is expected. The psychodynamic process of transference, a favorite of psychology-based programs, is considered to be the key mechanism that will work the "cure," as the child-client's old ideas give way under the influence of his new associations and his identification with a proper role model.[38]

There is perhaps a paradox in the juxtaposition of abstractions of psychodynamic theory and the realities of bureaucratic control systems. The staff of a typical remedial program is expected to "treat" the youth for his "own good" by removing him from the meaningful scenes of his childhood, by placing him in artificial groups of strangers assigned to be his "peers," by trying to argue down his self-understanding in therapies of all sorts, by detaching his significant loyalties in an attempt to replace environment, peers, understanding, and loyalties of the past with "better" ones chosen unilaterally by the alien helper-adult for reasons of his own. No matter what the child may have done to deserve this treatment, he may find it difficult to cope with this much control. His resentment may even be healthy. Yet the outlines of this process have not been questioned by the juvenile justice system itself, since it is intrinsically a system of "keepers and captives," as Jerome Miller points out, in which accountability of the dominant to the subordinate group has not been an issue.[39]

Release programs, such as parole and probation, tend to operate on the same assumptions, although in the client's own neighborhood. Technically qualified personnel engage in surveillance, in control, and in conditioning responses to the client, and professional counseling supports behavior "cures" that the officer has in mind for the client. The officer sets himself up in contrast and opposition to the client's home setting in which the criminogenic elements are alleged to be operating.

Elmer Johnson points out that the parole officer is different from his client in social class, education, and often race, yet expects to win support for parole objectives from the parolee and from third parties in the community.[40] His education has presumably provided him with a reservoir of facts and insights he can draw on as he applies his sanctioned rationality in the service of objectives that he and the parole system have for rehabilitating the client. Even if racial, religious, and ethnic qualities are shared with the client, the parole supervisor is usually not a member of the client's own community. A "stranger," through his personal characteristics he must become intimate with the client and strive to influence the parolee's behavior in ways consistent with rehabilitation goals. He expects to do this by being accepted as a role model. He acts as a confidential mediator between the client and members of the community in which the parolee must develop relatively new, rehabilitated relationships. The parole officer may, for example, help find a job for the client.

The parole or probation officer has authority over the client that does not derive from mutual experience and personal intimacy but rests on sources external to the worker-client relation. The professional worker is a visiting institutional functionary who is paradoxically expected to be a confidant to his client. The officer is independently powerful; the client is cast by the juvenile courts in the role of an involuntary dependent to whom the other does not have to listen. Yet identification with the worker, even transference, is counted on as the lever that will effect the requisite transformation in the faulty personality of the client.

Another variant of this approach is found in prevention and deterrence programs organized in recent years in which a worker is sent to focus a variety of diffuse efforts on the problems of youth and delinquency in a single community. The professionally trained, psychiatrically oriented adult worker is assigned to an area or a local group with a mandate to contact its members and to establish relations with them in order to change the resident gangs.

In a typical example reported by Walter Miller, workers saw their work as a series of sequential phases, on the model of individual psychotherapy.[41] First, close, "meaningful" relations were established with gang members as a major device for behavior change. On insinuating himself into the group, the worker is expected to see that mutual trust, mutual affection, and a pattern of reciprocal obligation develop between himself and the group members. Second, behavior modification is attempted by creating subgroups out of the membership of the local gang. The worker will involve everybody in organized clubs and sports to give the former gang members experience in participating in rule-governed activities and to make it necessary to maintain legitimate relations with elements of the adult community, inasmuch as club activities must be planned, halls rented, and so on.

In this and other contacts, such as those between the youths and the courts, the worker serves as intermediary between his clients and adult institutions. The services he performs to meet the "needs" of the youths are expected to enhance the client's respect for the worker and a feeling of reciprocal obligation. On the premise that the "devil makes work for idle hands," organized activities are also expected to curtail the time and energy available for unlawful activities. On the theory that youths take up delinquent activities because their access to legitimate channels in the adult world is blocked, the worker opens up such channels by involving community groups of adults with his projects, locating potential employers, and mediating between the youths and any adults with whom they may have problems.

The mechanism of change is expected to lie in the direct influence of a law-abiding middle-class adult who gives active support, through "subtle indirection" and "vigorous argument," to lawful values on a range of issues. Again, identification with the worker as a role model is expected in spite of differences in salient social characteristics between the worker and the youths. Techniques for manipulating group dynamics are also attempted by the worker in dealing with emergent situations that are openly discussed in group sessions. Indirect suggestion, nondirective leadership, permissive group guidance, and collective reinforcement are supposed to be used to implement changes in the individual members and in the values and attitudes they collectively express. Such changes are expected to alter the probabilities of future delinquency.

The third step in the psychiatrically oriented correctional process used by the detached social worker is, of course, the calculated withdrawal of the worker from the group, leaving the group to carry on within their rehabilitated ideas and relations.

In actual programs the client is, of course, not entirely powerless and dependent, however much the system chooses to render him so. Any inmate of a total control situation retains some ability to subvert the intentions of the program through an inner refusal to submit to coercion. Through dissembling, through manipulation of the worker, through withholding assent to the appeals and rewards of the program as well as to its threats, he can retain his own attitudes, especially if he has access to support from others in the program with whom he can identify more readily than he can with the professionals who run things.

Moreover, in actual programs young offenders are not really treated as though they were "sick." Indeed, the realities of day-to-day interaction are conditioned by the bureaucratic structure in which programs are carried out. Bureaucratic staff, concerned with accountability to superiors and with efficient execution of established procedures, are not readily able to incorporate into formal routines the differences of behavior and attitude that novel, theoretically grounded treatment may call for. The hopes that once attended the establishment of the juvenile court with power to assign cases to alternative treatments have been "bureaucratically" undone, says Walter Miller. Theoretical programs are transformed when interpreted into specific action. In addition, the old societal ambivalence—whether to treat or to punish—continues to affect the form of the programs. Aside from the failure of the "get tough" or correctional approach to accomplish much, there is an inherent political and social price to pay.

Model II   Experimental studies have been undertaken to test certain sociological theories about delinquent subcultures, on the assumption that if group values support and encourage delinquency, it is group values that must be changed.[42] This approach recognizes the intrinsic nature of the youth's membership in a delinquent system and treats him as a part of that system of group relations, not as a "sick" individual. Delinquent behavior is assumed to be primarily a group product, so that the group is conceived as the primary object as well as the primary means of treatment.

Typically the client does not reside in the controlled setting, but may be brought in from home to participate in a professionally composed and directed group that is intended to replace his delinquent associates as a reference group. The directed group is supposed to become the one whose standards he values and whose approval he hopes to win by conforming to group expectations. By removing the youth from the group structure that approved and reinforced his delinquency and by placing him in a group mediating and reinforcing the values of the society at large, it is hoped that the delinquent will switch his orientation. The structure of relations between group members and those who compose and guide the group is still an association of unequals, with authoritarian privilege sanctioned for the professional staff. The nature of control, however, is masked by the process of group encounter into which the youth is injected.

The mechanism of change on which this approach relies is the force of "cognitive dissonance." According to Leon Festinger, when a system of perception, belief, or other form of information comprises inconsistent items of knowledge about persons, events, situations, or objects, the individual experiences discomfort or tension that motivates him to reduce the dissonance by modifying one or more aspects of his cognitive system.[43] This feeling of dissonance is expected to emerge in the course of group interaction and to motivate change, reinforced by the pressure of the peer group.

Sponsors of this approach argue that the delinquent must be made anxious about the utility of the delinquent system of behavior and values. When the client switches his allegiance to the new group, group discussion can force him to deal with conflict between the delinquent system and the conventional one promoted by the staff interlocutor. The guidance is supposed to be indirect, while the group mentor waits for "wisdom" to emerge in the course of discussion. In the group meetings, reasons for delinquency must be examined and rejected. Free expression is encouraged to bring out debate on the conflict of norms, with the assumption that in free debate the conventional norms will win out. Any decision for or against conventional behavior must be seen as a community decision, in order to promote a change of reference group for the participators in this community. Every use is made of the ambivalent feelings that arise from the conflict of conventional and criminal norms.

Ideally, say its promoters, the social structure of this therapeutic community will consist of an effective, cohesive child-adult system devoted to one task: overcoming lawbreaking. The adult authorities must not seem to be "rejectors," a rule intended to head off the probable reaction in which the rejectors are rejected and with them the program itself. Opportunities must be provided for recognizing and rewarding conventional pursuits, while evasion of punishment for backsliding must be made impossible. The youth peer group formed in the treatment center should be seen as the primary source of help and support by participants (who are nevertheless a "captive clientele"). Transference and role modeling are not viewed as vital to change.

Certain categories of offenders are judged more likely to succeed in the program, and generally this means it is tried mostly with status offenders or with better educated, white, or middle-class youths who, on the evidence, are likely to "get better" no matter what is done for them. High-risk types, designated incorrigible, are kept out, thus helping to promote the probable rate of success of the therapy and, incidentally, to confirm the professional theory involved.

Examples of therapeutic approaches, based on the concept of group relations, include the Provo experiment (1965) in Utah[44] the Highfields group home experiment (since 1950) in New Jersey[45] and the Community Treatment Project (1961) in California.[46] For each of these model treatment programs, specific records measure the effectiveness of the program for reducing recidivism. In the case of the Provo treatment, a marked improvement was found in *both* the Provo and the control group (a reformatory) as measured on a previous rate of success, but the principle of group treatment could not be shown to be responsible for any of the improvement. The Highfields Project was residential and involved a shorter period of intensive treatment. Allocation to Highfields was selective rather than random, and results were compared with those from a similar group in a local reformatory. There was little evidence of change in attitude or personalities, and the general failure rate was as high for Highfields as for the reformatory. The Community Treatment Project, with random allocation of clients between the experimental and control groups, showed that after two years, fewer than four out of ten experimental clients, compared with six out of ten in an institution, had parole revoked.

Advocates of the group therapy approach say that often the courts are unwilling to risk allocating repeaters and those known to be deeply alienated and hostile, so that a true experimental test of the effectiveness of this approach is hard to achieve. Without truly random allocation of cases to control and experimental groups, it is said, the poor and uncertain performance of group-based therapy remains to be fully explained by research.

The effectiveness of mental health approaches to crime control has recently been questioned on several different grounds. For one, major social and economic differences between mental health providers and the recipients of their service affect the nature and out-come of treatment. Cultural and value differences between the professional and patient impinge on their interaction with each other in much deeper ways than mental health professionals like to admit. For another, serious questions are being raised within the mental health field itself about the lasting effects of treating individuals without regard to their family relationships and their abilities to function in their communities.

REFERENCES

1. The legislative bodies of the states of New York and Illinois recently low-ered the jurisdictional age limit to fourteen.
2. Robert L. Woodson, "A Review of the Office of Juvenile Justice Delin-quency Prevention, Prepared for the Judiciary Subcommittee on Crime, United States House of Representatives," 95th Congress, 2d session, November 1978.
3. Michael Smith, director of the Vera Institute, in prepared testimony before the U.S. Senate Judiciary Subcommittee to Investigate Juvenile Delinquency, April 11, 1978.
4. Franklin E. Zimring, "Confronting Youth Crime," in Twentieth Century Fund, *Task Force Report on Sentencing Policy toward Young Offend-ers* (New York: Holmes and Meier, 1978), p. 4.
5. Franklin E. Zimring, *Dealing with Youth Crime, National Needs and Priorities,* U.S. Department of Justice, Law Enforcement Assistance Ad-ministration, Office of Juvenile Justice, 1975.
6. Milton Lugar, former OJJDP assistant, stated in a staff memorandum: "Historically, as well as currently, the greatest incidence of crime and de-linquency is in urban areas . . . while private not-for-profit youth-serving agencies locate services in middle income and affluent communities."
7. Roger G. Hood, "Research on the Effectiveness of Punishments and Treat-ments," in Strasbourg Council of Europe, ed., *Collected Studies in Crimi-nological Research,* (Strasbourg, 1976).
8. L.T. Wilkins, "A Comparison Study of Results of Probation," *British Journal of Delinquency* 8 (1958): 201-9; D.V. Babst and J.W. Mannering, "Probation vs. Imprisonment for Similar Types of Offenders, A Com-parison by Subsequent Violations," *Journal of Research in Crime and Delinquency* 2 (1965); and P.F.C. Mueller, *California Board of Probation Study, Final Report,* Sacramento, 1965, pp. 90-6.
9. Roger G. Hood and Richard Sparks, *Key Issues in Criminology* (New York: McGraw-Hill, 1971), pp. 187-8.

10. Roger G. Hood, "Some Research Results and Problems," in Leon Radzinowicz and Marvin Wolfgang eds., *Crime and Justice,* vol. 3, (New York: Basic Books, 1971), p. 163.

11. Hood and Sparks, *Key Issues in Criminology,* p. 190; also, K. Berntsen and K. Christansen, et al, eds., Scandinavian Studies in Criminology (London, 1965), pp. 35-54.

12. A discussion of the point is found in Hood and Sparks, *Key Issues in Criminology,* p. 193, see also R.G. Hood, "Some Research Results," pp. 177-9.

13. W.C. Bailey, "Correctional Outcome and Evaluation of 100 Reports," *Journal of Criminal Law and Criminology in Political Science* 57 (1966): 153.

14. Robert Martinson, "What Works—Questions and Answers about Prison Reform," *Public Interest* 35 (Spring 1974): 22.

15. See Francis Allen, "Criminal Justice, Legal Values and the Rehabilitation Ideal," *Journal of Criminal Law, Criminology and Police Science* 50 (1959): 226.

16. Jerome G. Miller, *The Revolution in Juvenile Justice (From Rhetoric to Rhetoric)* (Gambier, Ohio: Kenyon Public Affairs Forum, 1978), pp. 7 and 8.

17. Ibid., p. 23.

18. Ibid.

19. Marvin Wolfgang, *Youth and Violence,* U.S. Department of Health, Education, and Welfare, Youth Development and Delinquency Prevention Administration, Social and Rehabilitation Service, 1970, p. 45.

20. Ibid., pp. 46-8.

21. Ibid., p. 45.

22. Ibid., p. 48.

23. Ibid., pp. 20-1.

24. Miller, *Revolution in Juvenile Justice,* p. 40 passim.

25. James Q. Wilson, *Thinking About Crime* (New York: Vintage Books, 1975), p. 59.

26. George Napper, "Perceptions of Crime Problems and Implications," in Robert L. Woodson, Ed., *Black Perspectives on Crime and the Criminal Justice System* (Boston: G. K. Hall, 1978), p. 9.

27. Charles Morgan, Jr., "Talking Sense about Crime," in *When the Marching Stopped* (Washington, D.C.: National Urban League, 1973), p. 60.

28. See Sarah Carey, ed., *Law and Disorder,* vol. 4 (Washington, D.C.: Center for National Security Studies, 1976).

29. See the evaluation of the District of Columbia preventive detention system in *Preventive Detention in the District of Columbia: The First Ten Months* by Nan C. Bases, Vera Institute of Justice, New York, and William F. McDonald, Georgetown Institute of Criminal Law and Procedure (Washington, D.C.: Vera Institute, 1972).

30. New York State Budget, 1977.
31. City of New York, Comptroller, Bureau of Municipal Investigation and Statistics, *Report on Foster Care Agencies, Achievement of Permanent Homes for Children in their Care,* no. E77-403, May 1977.
32. It should be noted that these problems are not confined to the private child welfare agencies, but are common throughout the child welfare system. For related studies, see *Children Without Homes* (Washington, D.C.: Children's Defense Fund, April 1977); David Fanshel and Eugene Shinn; *Children in Foster Care* (New York: Columbia University Press, 1978); and U.S. Congress, *Joint Hearings before the Subcommittee on Children & Youth,* 94th Congress, 1st session, December 1, 1975.
33. Nicholas Pileggi, "Who'll Save the Children?" *New York* (December 18, 1978): 53-6.
34. Kenneth Clark, "Community Action and the Social Programs of the 1960's," in David C. Warner, ed. *Toward New Human Rights: The Social Policies of the Kennedy and Johnson Administrations* (Austin: University of Texas, 1977), p. 97.
35. Lerone Bennett, *New York Amsterdam News* (August 12, 1976): editorial page.
36. Burton J. Bledstein, *The Culture of Professionalism* (New York: Morton Library, 1976).
37. *A Comparative Analysis of Delinquency Prevention Theory: Preventing Delinquency,* vol. 1, Working Papers (Washington, D.C.: National Task Force to Develop Standards and Goals for the Office of Juvenile Justice and Delinquency Prevention, 1977).
38. Walter B. Miller, "Preventing Delinquency," in Radzinowicz and Wolfgang, eds., *Crime and Justice,* vol. 3, p. 315.
39. See J. Miller, *Revolution in Juvenile Justice,* p. 53.
40. Elmer H. Johnson, "The Parole Supervisor in the Role of Stranger," *Journal of Criminal Law, Criminology and Police Science* 50 (May-June 1959: 38-43. Johnson concludes, however, that the fact that the parole officer is a "stranger" does not handicap the process of adjustment for the delinquent.
41. Walter B. Miller, "Preventing Delinquency," in Radzinowicz and Wolfgang, eds., *Crime and Justice,* vol. 3, pp. 313-35.
42. Model I approaches also may make use of group dynamics as they attempt to substitute an artificial therapeutic group for a "natural" but delinquent one. The difference is one of emphasis, Model I using an overall psychiatric orientation and Model II an orientation to small group theory.
43. On the concept of "cognitive dissonance," see Leon Festinger, *A Theory of Cognitive Dissonance* (Evanston, Ill.: Row-Peterson, 1957).
44. La Mar T. Empey and Jerome Rabors, "The Provo Experiment: Theory and Design," in Radzinowicz and Wolfgang, eds., *Crime and Justice,* vol. 3, p. 266.

45. For a complete report on Highfields, see H.A. Weeks, *Youthful Offenders at Highfields* (Ann Arbor: University of Michigan Press, 1958).

46. Marguerite Q. Warren, "The Community Treatment Project: History and Prospects," in S.A. Yefsky, ed., *Law Enforcement, Science and Technology* (Washington, D.C.: Thompson, 1967), pp. 191–200.

2 AN ALTERNATIVE APPROACH

Youths on the stage of juvenile justice find themselves assigned roles in a morality play in which the best parts are reserved for others. It stands to reason that defense of the self—through dissembling, resistance, subversion, and manipulation of all sorts—is the usual response to "treatment," even treatment administered with the best of intentions.

It is argued here that formal programs for delinquents fail in their attempts at "child saving" because of the way they are structured and staffed. The professionalism of workers, the artificiality of worker-client relations, and the disruption of the youth's primary ties to kin and kind and self inhibit the chance of development or change, especially among youths from more difficult worlds—those of marginal socioeconomic or minority status, from the inner city, the culturally deprived or alienated. These children are the hard-core delinquents, statistically responsible for a disproportionate share of the index crimes, whose rehabilitation would do the most for public safety and community development. Yet they will probably have less reason and ability as a group to make the large leap required to achieve appropriate middle-class identifications and to invest themselves deeply in the artificial relations held out.

THE NEIGHBORHOOD AS THE
BASIS FOR CHANGE

Hard-core delinquents and youths in risk of becoming so may indeed fall outside the competence of professional rehabilitation programs, as some professionals themselves suggest. But these youths can still be helped; many are being helped through indigenous inner city programs where a nonprofessional staff of volunteer neighbors works with delinquents, their families, and local groups and agencies for the development of the community. In these programs a structure of primary relations among members supports the possibility of cooperation and authentic mutual influence, as individual and community development proceed together.

The importance of primary bonding in any person-changing process must be stressed. Socialization and development are influenced by contact with other socialized beings. In this, conformity is never total, and individuals observe some norms and ignore others. But the desire to be with people in gratifying ways leads the individual to compromise, and the gratification from finding needs met through encounters with others and the development of emotional and practical interdependence increase the individual's willingness to modify the self in group-approved directions. In this, the family and peer groups are certainly fundamental influences. Behavior patterns transmitted to individuals through these groups are consistent with the total matrix of social and cultural conditions to which the norms of the group represent adaptations.

When trying to change or modify individual patterns of behavior that are in some way "deviant," it must be realized that any group of people with similar circumstances and a similar degree of access to culturally desirable rewards and activities will express similar needs and attitudes in similar life-styles. In the anonymity and pluralism of urban life, people who react to their life chances in much the same way will find each other; they will tend to interact primarily with one another and to reinforce the attitudes and patterns of behavior that typify their group. Changing deviant individuals therefore requires changing the conditions that call forth the deviant adjustment. The options appear to be (1) changing the social and economic conditions of the deviant's home place; (2) introducing him to a new place with a new matrix of life chances; (3) removing the individual from the support of the group that reinforces his deviant adaptation;

(4) supplying him with a new social group whose adaptive values and attitudes will serve to integrate his behavior into the new matrix of chances (usually conceived as those of the middle class); and finally (5) contriving that he *accept* the new group as a primary group with which he identifies, that is, from which he receives personally meaningful and gratifying responses and through the influence of which he is willing to reshape his basic cognitive and cathectic adaptations. Some of these conditions must be met in order to reconstruct successfully a deviant life-style. The only other possibility would be dramatic conversion to the appeal of a charismatic personality.

The difficulty, of course, is that these conditions inherently resist manipulation and present the controller with different kinds and degrees of resistance. The syncopated effectiveness of the juvenile justice programs for deterrence and reform testify to the difficulty. For example, in options 1 and 2, extensive and intensive reconstruction of criminogenic social conditions (as by urban reconstruction or war on poverty) brings reconstructors immediately into conflict with fundamental social and economic processes that undergird the whole society. The reconstructors cannot, for example, dismantle capitalism or arbitrarily redistribute people into less occupied sections of the country. They are confined to dealing piecemeal with one aspect after another of the social problems continuously generated by urban concentration, economic marginality, cultural pluralism, and relative social powerlessness.

Vocational training and efforts to keep people in school address themselves to option 2. If the individual could be reequipped to compete at a different level in the opportunity structure of society, it might draw him into a different complex of life chances. Unfortunately, education, though necessary, is not by itself sufficient to relocate the individual socially. Many other factors affect the chance of upward mobility, including the readiness of the individual himself to break off the emotional-cultural relations that have shaped his life to date. Other factors are racism, union priorities, and the general condition at any time of the nation's economy—its capacity to absorb cohorts of workers newly prepared to contend for positions. Many people in our social basement faithfully complete training only to find their actual life circumstances little altered.

The third and fourth options are generally relied on by the juvenile justice system in the modal its approaches to deviance. The power to remove individuals physically and to surround them with new associates is certainly available. The power to insinuate middle-class or "reformed" values into these artifically constructed groups is less available, and even less readily at hand is the power to contrive the "primariness" of the relations formed in the group. Least available of all is the willingness of those in forced subordination or forced propinquity to commit themselves believingly to an involuntary association and to submit themselves to authentic self-change.

The chance that anyone will genuinely subordinate learned adaptations to the influence of a new group and new norms depends on the degree to which the new group resembles or is in fact composed of already familiar people with whom the individual can readily find things in common. It seems probable that those with whom he may have associated all along—people from his own neighborhood, people of the same social, cultural, and economic circumstances—could gain entrance to his deeper personal feelings and strivings more readily than professional helpers drawn from other social categories, educational levels, or cultural orientations. The already familiar neighborhood people are also more readily accepted in psychodramas of self-renovation than similar but unchosen associates.

Moreover, inner city neighborhoods, where social and cultural identities are widely shared, have the potential for acting as true communities; that is, they are not mere aggregates of statistics of social problems and social disorganization. There is the strong possibility that the residents will come together in conscious awareness of shared problems and relationships, forming communities of interest. They recognize the commonality of their life chances and adaptive styles and accept the responsibility to advance the common good. The authentic sense of community can be activated through indigenous leadership, which is apparently not unusual since it shows up again and again in ghettos.

A basic problem faced by communities that would revitalize is the problem of juvenile delinquency. The harmful psychological and economic consequences of malicious mischief, gang violence, and crime perpetrated by neighborhood youths interact strongly with all other social problems of the area. Thus, whenever inner city communities create appropriate primary groups for neighborhood children, they also improve their chances of affecting other local problems.

The formation of primary bonds, in which people subjectively identify and are meaningfully identified, may be the central event in successful dramas of self-renovation and, fortuitously, in positive community revitalization. Community-based primary groups, more readily accepted than juvenile justice programs, can take on the functions historically assigned to families. They can mediate between the neighborhood and its youths and, in so doing, truly modify the young people, many of whom have been the scandal of juvenile justice programs.

Without doubt, much remains to be done to clarify the social process whereby the specific effects of rehabilitation and deterrence programs are produced. The process of control itself must be more thoroughly explored, and the matter is of some urgency, as many have pointed out. Certainly the general performance of existing Justice Department approaches remains discouraging, but the specific failure of the system to help the urban children of low socioeconomic and minority status is notorious. Devising an effective, appropriate way to keep these young Americans on the safe side of the law or to bring them back over when they get in trouble would be the single most important advance that the juvenile justice enterprise could make. In the most cautious appraisal, it would seem that if standard approaches are indeed showing only doubtful and limited effectiveness—and only when dealing with lesser offenders—any new programs that can show some positive effect (especially among those in the hard-core category) are worthy of attention and support.

COMMUNITY RESPONSE TO YOUTH VIOLENCE

In a major departure from the popular punitive-deterrence, child welfare, or mental health strategies, an alternative approach to the youth crime problem is proposed here. According to Weber and other sociologists, one can understand the dynamics of social problems by penetrating the motives, self-interpretations, and values of the actors in the problems under study.[1] This "inner understanding" is the basis of effective strategies to change behavior and is most readily achieved by community members themselves in neighborhoods where the problems occur. In other words, the chance for successful resolution of social problems is greater when those directly afflicted by the problems, the actors on the scene, initiate and monitor solutions.

Over the past decade, and currently at the American Enterprise Institute's Mediating Structures Project, programs and activities in several cities throughout the country have been studied in which community members themselves are using their own resources to deal with the problems of youth violence. The effectiveness of these neighborhood projects—yet to be measured by controlled research— is impressive. Assessment of the changes in individuals who had been marked down as incorrigible and hard-core delinquents by professionals is supported by the testimony of the individuals themselves. It is also supported by the testimony of the community leaders who watch over these programs, of neighbors whose lives and property have become measurably more secure, and most significantly by the word of welfare bureaucrats, the courts, and other juvenile justice professionals, who have begun to refer their own cases to these neighborhood groups. Youths who were once anathema to community stability have reversed roles and are now acting as protectors of their own neighborhoods. The successes appear to be based on principles of youth development associated with a strong sense of "family," binding together adult supervisors and the youths to be changed.

Neighborhoods and communities that may foster criminal character in youths also have many natural human resources that, if properly tapped, can be effective in addressing the community's most complex problems. A community can be a viable organism. When it suffers acute breakdown, it moves to fight off threats to its existence. For example, during the riots of the mid-1960s in Baltimore and Memphis, for three or four days violence was escalated by both police and community. Peace and calm were restored in three hours, however, once some community leaders came forward and were able to persuade the police and National Guard to withdraw long enough to enable them to counsel their peers on the implications of continued violence. Calm was restored and order prevailed. Unfortunately, indigenous leadership was ignored when programs were later designed to address some of the complaints of the neighborhood residents. Instead, government planners and professionals turned once again to the traditional system of delivering social services.

Community-based approaches to community crime are of particular, critical importance in view of the age of the juvenile offenders of most concern. Statistics show the high-risk offenders are eighteen to twenty years old, with a growing trend for even younger children to commit serious crimes against persons and property. Treatment of such young offenders seems most appropriate within their own communities, where persons already significant to them and intimate with them can be mobilized to provide the control and support crucial to their reform. Here the role of outside assistance would be to aid, not to direct, the families and communities in fulfilling these responsibilities.

Where outside professional help is nonintrusive and is limited to supportive assistance to programs totally conceived and operated by community groups directly in touch with the problem, the young people treated become an integral part of both identifying and solving the problems. They are coequals in activities that meet their own needs for achievement and recognition and that give positive reinforcement to socially approved behavior.

This model for a juvenile program assumes that young offenders' needs extend far beyond the provision of jobs, education, and housing. Strong, healthy social values and respect for self and for human worth are often incompletely developed in inner city youths and certainly in delinquents. They need guidance of the kind advocated by the Reverend Jesse L. Jackson, founder and director of Operation PUSH (People United to Save Humanity), who contends that the youth problem includes much more than socioeconomic factors. He observes, "Our children are living in depressed neighborhoods and are on the verge of ethical collapse." He further advises that "morally weak people not only inhibit their own personal growth, but finally contribute to the politics of decadence . . . . A generation of people lacking the moral and physical stamina necessary to fight a protracted civilizational crisis is dangerous to itself, its neighbors and to future generations."[2]

Programs for the control of delinquent and criminal behavior must begin with strategies for the development and repair of the social attitudes of the youths in question. Reverend Jackson's national organization has recently launched Project EXCEL to encourage urban youngsters to make a personal commitment to excellence.[3] Program goals are to increase youth participation in community services, to lower school dropout rates, to expose young people to a variety of career options, and to provide strong, ethical behavioral models for youths to live up to. The strong support of parents and community members is viewed as critical to the success of the program, especially in efforts to encourage good work habits and good personal behavior.

THE SURROGATE FAMILY AND
YOUTH DEVELOPMENT

Functionally, the institution of the family has been society's basic support system for the development of personally adequate individuals, oriented to appropriate social values and capable of sustained, socially appropriate behavior. Under normal conditions, the natural family is the first and primary source of ethical, moral, and spiritual values in every individual. An extensive literature in social science documents the course of personality breakdown as a result of the family's incapacity or failure to serve developmental needs of its members. Young people from troubled families and neighborhoods, deprived of an appropriate learning milieu, often turn to street corner peer groups as sources of values, and as models of approved behavior.

My studies, presented in this volume, of inner city communities and violent youth gangs have revealed that successful community approaches to these youths are based on the spontaneous understanding among nonprofessional community members of the incapacity of the natural families to function adequately for their children. In each case, a family-like role structure seems to have been introduced within a group of local leaders and youths, and this surrogate family has provided the youths with effective primary social relations. Making use of already existing group ties, a positively oriented reference group composed of volunteers from the community has been substituted for the inadequate natural families and the street corner groups of violent, crime-oriented peers. These substitute families have not sought to discredit natural families in any way, but rather to support and augment them through efforts to build a contact environment for troubled youth conducive to their reorientation.

Many of the youths under study come from urban, minority families that differ greatly in structure from the average American family.

Niara Sudarkasa at the University of Michigan observes that among nuclear families, household and family are often coterminous, but among blacks, family and household are not usually equated. Without implying any functional disorganization, Sudarkasa writes: "Families cut across household divisions, and in many instances single households are only part of larger family structures. One of the important implications of this fact is that census data collected for individual households cannot be taken as the most important source of information on black family organization."[4] Sudarkasa further contends that "Among blacks, households centered around consanguineal relatives have as much legitimacy as family units as do households centered around conjugal unions."[5]

Robert Hill, director of research with the National Urban League, confirms and adds to this analysis. In a study of informal adoption among black families, Hill finds:

> About three million children, almost half of whom are black, currently live in households of relatives, while millions more reside with relatives for shorter periods of time as a means of providing low-cost day care services for working parents. . . .
> One of the key functions performed by the black extended family is the informal adoption and foster care of children by grandparents, aunts and uncles and other kin.[6]

The widespread acceptance of this form of family living among American blacks suggests the adaptive function it serves. Researcher John H. Scanzoni reports: "Partly because of structural conditions largely beyond their control, black persons face difficulties that are enormous in functioning in the white world. Similarly, the difficulties blacks face are enormous in maintaining a dominant-type conjugal family pattern."[7]

Elmer Martin, also commenting on the subcultural development of black extended families, found that the members are bound together by numerous ties of mutual obligation within which all the important functions of ideal conjugal families can be realized. The black extended family network can successfully provide family members with a humanly important sense of family solidarity and identity, allocating scarce family resources for the care of dependent family members, bestowing status and esteem on one another, defining the boundaries of deviant and immoral behavior, and teaching basic survival skills for dealing with hostile environments that may typically confront such "families."[8] Robert Hill makes a similar comment in his monograph *The Strengths of Black Families:* "Black families that have been extensively subjected to racial segregation and discrimination often characteristically show 1) strong kinship bonds, 2) strong work orientation, 3) adaptability of family roles, 4) strong achievement orientation and 5) strong religious and spiritual orientation."[9]

The substitution of an extended-family group for the nuclear, conjugal family is clearly a widespread adaptive response among American blacks to the stresses of their socioeconomic position. Although functionally inadequate families occur and continue to contribute to the influences bringing youths into criminal careers, the model of caring networks of people, associated as if they were true families, is firmly established among these populations and is perhaps more easily invoked and brought into play than many scholars realize. The extended surrogate family form is the structural basis of the youth control programs that are proposed here as a strong alternative to present juvenile justice approaches.

The conscious and deliberate family structure of these neighborhood youth development projects is providing effective, active support for the young people involved. The "family" lives in its own familiar neighborhood, where it can make maximum use of available human and material resources. Thus, an individual member of this unit is brought into direct relation through the family with the larger community structure, becoming actively involved with community development as an aspect of his own development.

This membership in a supportive family unit, positively coordinated with community values and institutions, takes on strategic importance for youths who have experienced only the alienation and threats of having to contend alone in a highly demanding, often hostile, social milieu. In their new families they acquire a new positive identity through participation in the families goals and struggles. This experience is reinforced through the mutual aid—the giving and receiving of help and counseling—that characterizes these functional extended "families."

It is argued here that if incomplete socialization is a major problem with delinquent youth, the necessary moral bond to society can be most effectively invoked in young people through their participation in the primary relations of family life. The community project taken as an analytical model for youth development through family control is a group in Philadelphia's ghetto known as the House of Umoja. In Umoja the basic family structure that outlines daily projects and secures the commitment of members is particularly clear and well developed—and successful. Like similar youth projects, it also stimulates the development of the host community. The presence of a family youth project, conceived and sponsored by non-professional, neighborhood adults, seems to encourage through its constructive activities the improvement of community relations generally and to call out local skills and resources for addressing other local problems.

CONCLUSION

Despite the evidence that "get tough" deterrence and child welfare and mental health strategies are not reaching a significant population of troubled youth, the courts have relied on these approaches to control violent youth crime, mostly after adjudication. In recent years, even prevention strategies have been channeled through the firmly established systems of professional youth service bureaus. Yet the incidence of recidivism and the impact of violent crime in inner city communities remain largely unaffected by these programs.

A more effective approach to problems of juvenile delinquency lies in the most basic institution of human society—the family. The more we rely on strategies that do not address youth problems through the family unit, the more we deceive ourselves about solutions and the true nature of the problem. Unfortunately, as ill-conceived strategies fail to produce the desired results, we seem to lose faith in any possible solutions.

The family, neighborhood, and community-based organizations are mediating structures, which offer new approaches to public understanding and new knowledge of the delivery of youth services that is sure to benefit the entire society. To make proper use of these indigenous resources requires, of course, a painful rethinking of the way public policy is developed. It is time to move in a different direction—toward a realization that some of the answers to mental health, crime, and other social enigmas already exist within the neighborhoods themselves and within their indigenous institutions, both formal and informal.

In light of these considerations, the House of Umoja, an outstanding example of community-based youth control, is presented as a timely alternative to existing resources of juvenile justice. Umoja is dealing effectively with children most in need of attention and least understood, from incipient delinquents to those deeply involved in violent, criminal street life. In addition, Umoja is not merely affecting the chances of local urban youth; its activities reach out into the community in positive ways. Umoja and its program function to combat anonymity, indifference, hopelessness, and other ills endemic to inner city life by putting local groups and institutions in touch with one another, by calling out latent indigenous resources of the community, and by drawing people together in collective efforts toward a shared purpose.

REFERENCES

1. In a recent private discussion of the point with me, Dr. Peter Berger made the following comment: "There are basically two approaches to the study of human social life. One can study 'hard facts,' such as those embodied in statistics. In this case we are studying society as a phenomenon outside the consciousness of individuals. Or we can study social life from within—that is, as experience that is interpreted and given meaning by those who go through it." See also, Julian Freund, *Max Weber* (New York: Pantheon, 1968), pp. 48-59. See especially Weber's concept of *verstehende Erklarung.*
2. Jesse L. Jackson, "A Challenge to the New Generation," *Ebony Magazine* (August 1978).
3. "Project EXCEL: More Funds Provided," *HEW Employees Newsletter* (July–August 1978): 1.
4. Niara Sudarkasa, "An Exposition of the Value Premises Underlying Black Family Studies," *Journal of National Medical Association* v. 67, no. 3 (August 16, 1972): 237.
5. Ibid., p. 238.
6. Robert B. Hill, *Informal Adoption among Black Families* (Washington, D.C.: National Urban League, 1977).
7. John H. Scanzoni, "Introduction and Perspective," in *The Black Family in Modern Society* (Boston: Allyn and Bacon, 1971), p. 2.
8. Elmer Martin, "A Descriptive Analysis of the Black Extended Family" Ph.D. diss., Case Western Reserve University, June 1975.
9. Robert B. Hill, *The Srengths of Black Families* (New York: Emerson Hall, 1972), pp. 3-39.

3 THE HOUSE OF UMOJA: A CASE STUDY

Philadelphia, Pennsylvania, has been plagued with youth gang violence for several decades, earning an unenviable reputation as the Youth Gang Capital of America. Each year an average of thirty-nine black youths died on the streets, and hundreds more were maimed for life.[1] Innocent bystanders were often felled by stray bullets when caught in a crossfire. As gang warfare raged, the general crime rate continued to soar, and many residents of the city's black community feared to leave their homes during the day. At night muggings of the young and old alike were common occurrences. Retail businesses closed before sundown, leaving steel gates to defend against potential intruders.

The tree-lined streets of West Philadelphia declined rapidly, as did other large city neighborhoods, with the withdrawal of small businesses, boarded-up houses, and massive removal of entire blocks of dilapidated houses. One factor contributing to the decline was crime and the fear that it would spread.

In the late seventies the scene began to change, however. From 1976 to 1979 there was a marked drop in the number of gang deaths in Philadelphia. The crime rate is now slowly abating,[2] and West Philadelphia is coming back to life as plans are being devised to restore areas of the city. Two leaders in this change are David and Falaka Fattah, founders of the House of Umoja, a nonprofessional neighborhood organization. With unorthodox ideas and no formal training in social work, they have taken in and embraced some of Philadelphia's toughest gang members in a new concept of peace. The efforts of the Fattahs have been rewarded as the number of gang deaths in the city declined from an average of thirty-nine deaths per year to six in 1976 and to just one death in 1977.

This book's report of the House of Umoja evolved over three years of observation, consultation, and work with members of the family. The story was constructed from notes, interviews, discussions, and in-depth study of the persons and activities at Umoja. The importance of this case for the larger national problem of youth crime was examined after a long assessment of the problems Umoja addressed and the internal resources utilized by all members of this extended family.

The positive outcome of Umoja's work with young gang members in Philadelphia has convinced me that this model of self-help among neglected, abused, and potentially violent youths can be replicated in similar problem areas throughout the nation. This chapter is devoted to a descriptive analysis of the Umoja approach to solving problems of troubled youths, who once presented for Philadelphia some of the most serious threats to social order on record.

ORIGINS OF THE HOUSE
OF UMOJA

Sister Falaka Fattah is a warm, pleasant, and affable person who looks younger than her mid-forties. Her conversation is sprinkled with constant reference to the "kids," and she often adjusts her language to speak in the vernacular to youngsters seeking information or advice. A print chiffon scarf on her head complements her long African-style dress. Both she and her husband David prefer to use African terms as a cultural reference.

According to Falaka, Umoja was largely inspired by her own extended family. She recalled stories about relatives who had done various things to help black people. Falaka felt a special kinship toward these relatives and was moved to help black people herself. She also tells of earlier in her life planning to write a book with a friend entitled *Design for Good Living*.[3] The proposed book was to stress the importance of the family as the basic social institution through which a sense of stability is gained and values are transmitted. Concerned specifically with problems of youth and believing that society as a whole was responsible for the juvenile delinquency in her community, Falaka envisaged helping youths through a community- and government-supported recreation center that would be "a combination of children's hotel, restaurant, night club, sports arena, study hall, and forum."

David Fattah is an intelligent, friendly, and at times extremely intense person who has strong attachments to and knowledge of the plight of young blacks in the streets. As a former gang member who grew up in Philadelphia, David is one of the few adults who enjoys the complete trust and confidence of gang members from different parts of the city. His street savvy combines with his academic training at Temple University where he has been studying business administration. His training is on-again, off-again because being surrogate father to the residents of Umoja has interfered with his education.

The Fattahs, like other parents in Philadelphia, were continually concerned about the daily slaughter of young black people in gang warfare on the city's streets. Their concern was intensified in 1969 when they learned that the eldest of their six sons was a fringe member of a street gang called Clymer Street. The youth gang problem in Philadelphia was so acute at the time that the *Philadelphia Inquirer* dubbed 1969 "The Year of the Gun."

As the violence increased, gang membership increased, often as a result of the most insidious means of recruiting. Youths throughout the city who had managed to avoid the gang scene soon found their situation tenuous, their lives threatened, their money extorted in school cafeterias, their property stolen or destroyed until membership was agreed upon. Using scare tactics such as these, gang leaders encountered few obstacles as they rampaged through the schools and the neighborhoods, vandalizing the already decaying streets. Parents throughout the city remained in constant fear for the lives of their children. Simple functions such as grocery shopping became a flirt with danger.

Philadelphia, like most other urban cities, has, at best, minimal recreational facilities for its low-income youth. Those who can, use the YMCA and other such places. But the majority of potential gang recruits must burn off their high adolescent energy on crumbling city basketball courts, on baseball fields strewn with broken glass and litter, or on a street corner (in the parlance of the street, "just hanging out").

In the words of one young House of Umoja resident:

Fighting and fighting and fighting. Like, I was from a little gang when I was little. You grow up in the wrong neighborhood, you meet some gang, you have to fight every day. Well, it was just like you had to go to school, and gangs—they were just fighting. And I had to come back home, and I had to fight. I couldn't get the right education because I had to fight so many brothers before. I couldn't do any work for this fighting. I got in arguments with my mom because my school situation was bad, and that was because I was fighting in school every day.

But I had to fight or get beat up. I had to protect myself. Then I had got so used to fighting that as soon as somebody would say something to me, I was calling them out for a fight. And I just mixed in with the crew. And after that I couldn't get an education, so they kicked me out of school.

After long hours of consultation with their son and the fifteen youths in the gang, the Fattahs extended an invitation to the group to come and live with them. Sister Fattah relates that the only commitment they made to the young people was to help them stay alive and to keep them out of jail. All the youths were between the ages of fifteen and seventeen. The leader (or runner) was being hunted by a rival gang. The police, too, were searching for him. So David and Falaka Fattah, their six sons, and an elderly mother made room in their small, four-room house. Virtually all the furniture in the house had to be removed to accommodate mattresses that were used for both sleeping and sitting. Falaka Fattah began to teach the boys English, and David began coaching them in mathematics and economics. They also relied on television as a teaching tool. Role playing was used at first to prepare them for job interviews and court appearances. After a year, Sister Fattah said, "We were all alive, and no one went to jail, nor did any of the youngsters want to go home."

In June 1969, before the establishment of Umoja, David Fattah took to the streets to find our firsthand what the street gangs were like and to determine their motivations. Calling upon his own gang background, he spent months lounging around the street corners, pool rooms, and bars, visiting hospital emergency rooms to see youths injured during their frequent battles, and attending funerals of gang members. Some of the insights gained in the process later proved helpful, for example, in preventing more deaths, which often occurred in hospitals.

When David had been an active gang member, hospitals were safe havens, sanctuaries against intrusion. He found, however, that in 1969 gang members in Philadelphia declared no quarter (or no cuartel). Once an injured gang member was taken to a hospital, his opponents would often break into the emergency room, push aside physicians and nurses, and begin ripping the tubes from the patient's arms; bandages were torn from newly covered wounds. Friends and allies of the youth would fight back with fists, bottles, and other objects in this new battle zone. Hospital security guards were forced to call for reinforcements from the city's police, many of whom had quelled the initial disturbance. Several youths died as a result of such attacks.

David learned that funerals were favorite recruitment grounds for new gang members, as friends and relatives gathered to mourn the death of a youth. Solemnity mixed with tears and aggressive rage found final expression in a call for revenge that meant only one thing, "A body for a body." Payments of the claim from the rival "corner" (another name for gang) would have to await another day, as the mourning period would extend throughout the night with the drinking of wine in commemoration of the deceased youth.

David believed that one factor contributing to group conflict was black migration to the North from southern towns and cities. He discussed the historical growth of the problems as follows: The migration had disturbed family life and communal traditions. People from certain states tended to move into the same areas of the city. Soon there were family feuds and vendettas against people living in different areas, which eventually evolved into fights between gangs with defined boundaries, or "turfs." For decades in Philadelphia, hostilities and resentments of one generation were passed on to the next. It was not uncommon for grandchildren to belong to the same gang as their grandfather had. In successive generations the number of gang deaths increased with the availability of sophisticated weapons and the youths' impoverished sense of their own worth. David believes that television violence is a major influence in the lives of the youths. Gangster movies were the most popular—in fact, 70 percent of the 300 gang members surveyed by David had nicknames like "Dutch" and "Scar Face," taken from the Elliott Ness television show, "The Untouchables."[4] These characters served as role models.

David also talked with the parents and teachers of the youths to gain their thoughts and impressions of the plight of the youths and to learn something of the stresses faced by each group. Many boys were questioned in private, away from peers with whom they must constantly posture. David's reputation of being tough when he was on the streets brought him credibility among the gang members. This made his task of gathering information much easier. When consulted about the cause of youth crime in Philadelphia, he defined it as the disruption of family traditions and the families' inability to meet the needs of the youths. David Fattah also concluded that the youngsters' parents were acting out their frustrations in response to a neglectful and sometimes hostile environment. Some of the homes in which the children grew up were disorganized and loosely supervised by parents who were themselves struggling to survive burdensome lives. The youths found security, acceptance, and an element of defined expectation in the gang—an environment they understood and one that understood them. Disillusionment and despair had long since taken root in the minds and hearts of these youngsters. The creation of Umoja and its extended family was seen as a solution to this scenario by David and Falaka.

The youths were encouraged by Sister Falaka to organize along the lines of the African extended family, a concept that she believes gives them the same emotional and material security as the street gang. The group gathers early each morning to discuss work assignments and problems of the day and often help each other by role playing to prepare for outside activities, such as job interviews.

For some of the youths, it was not easy to adapt to an organized family life-style. Some were ravaged by street war and forced to be in constant motion to survive. Nights for some were spent wherever someone offered shelter. Parents who cared had difficulty contending with the erratic and often unpredictable behavior of their children. The youths' behavior was typified by the comments of a Umoja resident:

Like, say, my friends—right—I'd be with them all the time. And they said they would let me stay over at their crib [house]. Right. So, about 1:00 or 2:00 o'clock in the morning, or something, I would stop and they'd tell me I can't stay over at their crib. It happened all the time. I would be like, sitting out, you know, waiting for daylight to come.

SANCTUARY

Despite some of the early difficulties, the fifteen original members all remained throughout the first year. A code of conduct was established, based on a set of principles that amounted to a constitution. It helped the youths adjust and guided the conduct of daily life at the house. "Umoja," a Swahili word meaning "unity within the family," is made up of seven principles:

1. Unity of self
2. Unity within the family
3. Unity within the House of Umoja
4. Unity within the neighborhood
5. Unity within the black community
6. Unity with black people in the world
7. Unity in the area of human rights for all people

There are both rigid scheduling and a maximum of free time, a planned course of action juxtaposed with freedom of choice, at the House of Umoja. Residents are taken under the authority of parents and siblings, who set limits and controls; each youth's personal qualities and unique problems are also recognized.

If a young person is to compete in the world of work, his time frame must be consistent with that of the work place. Gang youths are night people—rising late and staying up most of the night. To reorder this frame of reference, Umoja adheres to a rigid daily schedule. At 6:00 everyone rises with the sun. A conference is held to set goals for the day, to discuss the personal problems of the previous day, and to reach current decisions. Between 7:00 and 7:30 breakfast is served, the youths having an opportunity to choose from a limited menu. The rest of the morning is spent at school or work. From 3:00 in the afternoon to 10:00 at night, time is provided for the fulfillment of personal goals, such as homework and personal friendships.

Every Friday night the entire group meets in the evening for the Adella, a session similar to a tribal council but in which more traditional mental health circles would be called group therapy. This is a weekly review to resolve personal conflicts and settle disputes within the family. Any member may lead the discussion. Anyone found in violation of the canons of behavior, must name his own punishment. If they think the sanction too lenient, the group is free to suggest a more just punishment. The most severe sanction is to tell others on the street that the youth is not a person of his word. Even with the Adella, there are times when an individual problem must be handled one-to-one, usually with Sister Fattah.

Both the Adella and the individual counseling sessions are always conducted in the kitchen around food. Sister Fattah relates that the children of Umoja seldom have had enough food. Since food symbolizes nurturance, she makes certain that there is always enough food on hand; her theory: "Young people will fight when they are drinking together, but they will seldom fight when eating together."

As word spread about the House of Umoja, more and more youngsters sought sanctuary. The doors of the house were never locked, and on some mornings a new child would be found asleep on the floor. Seven more gang members asked to join the family, agreeing to stop gang warring (one of the first conditions for entry). Sister Fattah refused to turn any of the youngsters away, which imposed a burden on dwindling resources. The need for more space was immediately apparent. When the house adjacent to them was put up for sale, the entire family decided to try to purchase it. The Urban Coalition, a business-supported human service agency, awarded a grant of $1,500 to be used as a down payment on the $5,000 purchase price. The balance of the mortgage was to be paid over fifteen years. The house was soon filled by the new arrivals. Each member of the family contributed to the payment of the mortgage. Fund-raising events included block parties and rent parties. As a result, the youngsters repaid the fifteen-year mortgage in less than three years. With the help of local church groups and other civic organizations, a third property was purchased, enabling the Fattahs to accommodate many new arrivals as word of the Umoja program spread. A fourth and then a fifth house were added, until the House of Umoja owned twenty-two properties in various states of repair. The dwellings were all repaired by the residents. Seven are used as offices.

When the House of Umoja had exhausted its funds, it turned to the one neighborhood institution with a tradition of assisting those in need—the church. From the beginning, the church proved a friend to the Umoja cause. Members of the Philadelphia Council of Black Clergy, clergymen with a high degree of black consciousness and dedicated to the principle of directly assisting their black brothers and sisters, provided money and food. Neighborhood churches, white as well as black, also assisted Umoja in their own small way. Although the Fattahs were not Catholic or, for that matter, Christian, the Catholic church welcomed their program, saying that they were indeed fulfilling a Christian ethic by feeding, clothing, and providing shelter to needy children.[5] The Catholic church asked its parishioners—who were predominantly from the suburbs rather than the inner city—to donate a few groceries to the Umoja family. The response was immediate and abundant.

So much food was received that the members of Umoja were unable to store it all in their limited cabinet and refrigerator space. The Catholic church asked that any surplus food collected be distributed by Umoja throughout the community, and the residents began giving it away to children in the neighborhood as well as to friends and relatives. News of the free food spread quickly; the service was instrumental in bringing community residents together with the Umoja inhabitants. A Umoja boy's knock at the front door offering free canned goods was often the first contact between the two neighbors, even though they lived on the same block. People invited to the house to pick up the goods met the Fattahs.

Yet there was still some skepticism. For one thing, the Umoja family had hung a flag outside its front door that sported the vibrant, militant colors of the black Americans' link to a new Africa—black, red, and green. The only others in Philadelphia at the time who were exhibiting such colors and running a free food program were the Black Panthers, who, for many different reasons, were viewed with suspicion by some. Some residents therefore decided the House of Umoja and the Black Panther party were allied and informed the police.

The House of Umoja was not unfamiliar to the Police Department, which showed concern about a home full of delinquent gang members. The Umoja family could sense that the house was under surveillance. Young men living in the house were harassed by police, who were suspicious of the organization. Upon returning from school many were subjected to searches by police officers; others were arrested on suspicion of conspiracy to break the law. On one occasion cars belonging to visitors were towed away.

The Fattah family helped overcome this suspicion by inviting the local precinct captain, along with the officers who patrolled the Umoja neighborhood, to visit the House of Umoja. The police and the young people engaged in many exchanges, and tension between them lessened as understanding developed. Relations between the police and the House of Umoja varied, however, and old hostilities were occasionally revived. After a robbery or some minor outbreak of violence in the city, a rumor that Umoja's residents were responsible often resulted in renewed random searches and arrests of the youths in the neighborhood of the House of Umoja. Sister Fattah and a delegation from the house would again visit the local precinct captain to address this grievance. Some of the captains were very supportive and responsive to attempts to aid the area youth. One police captain referred job requests to the house, and twenty-five youths were once employed to assist in setting up a circus that had come to town. Each time the precinct's captain was transferred, the harassment would be renewed and negotiations would begin again. Because of these minor setbacks, the police and Umoja continued to have a precarious relationship. The older, more experienced youths at the house played a vital role in maintaining some rapport with the police.

With thirty young men living at the house and full participants in the extended kinship community, the Fattahs called upon the original fifteen to provide guidance to the newcomers. They aided in stabilizing the younger, more tempestuous youths who joined the family and were admired and respected.

Every new youth accepted into Umoja starts at the bottom, in accordance with the general policies that have been in effect since the opening of its doors. As the youth demonstrates his capacity to control himself and shows that he is dependable and trustworthy, his status improves, which usually means a better job and increased responsibility. He cannot achieve this new status simply by remaining in the program; he must aggressively pursue positive goals and self-improvement within the philosophical framework of Umoja's seven principles. Successful completion of the seven steps earns the youth the much sought-after prize—the right to change his last name to Fattah.

Names among gang youths are extremely important. Most youths who enter Umoja have street names such as Shotgun, Killer, or Snake which usually reflect some customary action by the person during battles or a concise statement of his personality. Nicknames are also used to identify some physical or mental handicap, such as a lame leg or a harelip. Labeling the youngsters in this fashion has the effect of minimizing the harassment the child may undergo. Constant reference to the malady detracts from any physical or psychological difference. If a youngster who is lame is constantly referred to as "Crip," it is forgotten that the name refers to a deformity, and thus the youth's difference is minimized. (The single exception to this rule is use of the name "Crazy" or "Craz," usually given only to someone severely disturbed and capable of unprovoked violence. Often such youngsters are avoided by the group or otherwise ostracized.)

A youth at Umoja is also able to earn his "Fattah" if he performs some heroic act on behalf of the community. One youth, for instance, attempted to persuade his gang to stop fighting and join the House of Umoja. For his efforts he was scorned by the gang and accused of cowardice, the greatest of all sins. The youth was stabbed severely as he was about the leave the neighborhood. From his hospital bed, he learned that his gang was about to engage in a large battle with another group that had invaded its turf. The youngster left his hospital bed and returned to his corner, appealing once again to his group to lay down their arms and come talk to Sister Fattah. The gang members were so moved by the courage exhibited by this young person that they eventually came to the house and pledged peace, recognizing that their comrade in arms was not motivated by fear, but by a call to life.

At a family reunion every year, each youth who has earned his name is honored in an elaborate ceremony during Kwanza (an African feast celebration, which occurs between December 26 and January 1). A civil official often performs weddings on this occasion in keeping with the Kwanza tradition.

The new Fattahs maintain their kinship with the house long after they graduate and leave. Often furloughs from military service are spent "back home." New fathers bring their children back for visits to the house, just as they would return to a nuclear family. The "leaving of the home" is also an important element in the evolution of the reconstituted lives of the youngsters that Umoja serves. The residential population is consciously limited to thirty youngsters at one time so as not to foster dependency. It is believed, moreover, that thirty is the maximum number that will permit the group to maintain its psychological integrity as a family. The thrust of Umoja is not to grow and expand as an institution, but to influence others in the community to embrace the spirit of the seventh and highest principle of Umoja: "Unity with human rights for all people."

In furtherance of this objective, Umoja's young people have spread the message of peace not only in the immediate neighborhood but also in the entire city of Philadelphia through programs of advocacy and community service. Each youth who comes to the house is assigned the responsibility of caring for and providing some service to other children in the immediate neighborhood. Some 270 of these children are served by Umoja residents on any single day. For many of the gang youths and others who have lived troubled lives, it is the first time they have been given the opportunity to be a provider of human service instead of a recipient. For example, a resident of Umoja who reads at the sixth-grade level may be asked to tutor a youngster who reads at the fourth-grade level, or he may be assigned to participate in or coach a recreational activity.

That Umoja fills the empty lives of young people is indicated by the following statements of residents:

> And there's a lot more people here all the time than it would be, like, on a regular block, see? These brothers here, they sleep together, they eat together—a good thirty of them. All of them want to eat together, play baseball together, you know. Other kids, they only got around one or two brothers. Every brother around here, he got umpteen brothers.
>
> Hey, at the House of Umoja you'll never find a lonely brother in this house. You always got somebody you can talk to, you know, any time you got a problem or something. Like, say, when you only got two sisters and they go out, and you got something you want to talk about, you have to really wait until they come back; where, here, you got somebody that you could talk to.
>
> There's always somebody here you can talk to. If you got any problem, you can talk to them, especially the Fattahs. That's what the Fattahs' job is, to help these brothers out when they have things on their mind that they're trying to get straight, and they need some help, need some kind of guidance.

Programs grew at the house as the needs was felt. In the beginning, wages earned by the boys from odd jobs were the only supplement to the income of the Fattahs. Thanks to the Catholic church, food was plentiful, but there were other needs that required funds. The young men began the awesome task of job hunting to help alleviate the need for money. But job hunting was much more than most of them had bargained for. Many of the young men lacked high school diplomas, having dropped out well before graduation. Many of them had never held a legitimate job. At first the youngsters went out on job interviews with little or no preparation and would appear at downtown office buildings wearing their street paraphernalia: "cool caps," earrings, dungarees, and tee shirts. Needless to say, employment was not forthcoming. In their frustration the youths came up with the idea of a job clinic where they would teach one another basic articulation and English language skills and participate in self-development and debating classes. They collectively decided that when a brother was granted a job interview, everyone else in the House would lend him a piece of clothing so that the brother going on the interview would be the best dressed person coming out of the House of Umoja that day. Cool caps and earrings were abandoned, and street talk was minimized.

These employment strategies paid off. The Umoja brothers started getting jobs, slowly, one by one. As increased revenue flowed into the house, a two-sided bulletin board was established—one side for "needs," the other for "wants." Needs were classified as essential items such as food and telephone and electric service. Wants were the personal items desired by the brothers, such as cigarettes or wine. After the needs of the house were met, the brothers' individual wants were addressed. The residents collectively began to feel responsible for all of the undertakings of the house. When the phone company threatened to shut off service, Sister Fattah and the young men went down to the company to plead their case. Sister Fattah called this their introduction to corporate responsibility. When executives at Bell Telephone heard their case and the history of their efforts, they were genuinely interested. Bell Telephone and the House of Umoja became immediate friends, and Bell often lent financial support to Umoja's programs. The company had previously been plagued by young vandals who frequently defaced and destroyed service trucks as they went through the community. When word got around that Bell Tel was "cool" and sympathetic to the efforts of Umoja, there was an appreciable decline in the vandalism of service trucks.

For the first time in their lives, the young men living at the House of Umoja felt they belonged to something. They worked together and achieved the structure that they had all been missing and that Sister Fattah had been hoping to achieve—a family.

RECOGNITION FROM THE CRIMINAL JUSTICE AND SOCIAL WELFARE SYSTEMS

Many of the residents of Umoja were clients of several probation officers. When the probation officers came looking for the youths, parents and friends would direct them to the House of Umoja.

After investigating, the officers found that those living at the house presented less of a problem than they had previously.

Although the probation officers would continually come and check on the youths, they would frequently leave with little, if any, contact with the staff of Umoja. One probation officer, however, felt particularly impressed with the program at the house. He was responsible for a young man who had been in and out of thirteen group home and institutional facilities, the last being the Camp Hill Detention Center, a maximum security prison for juveniles. The court felt that this probationer was in desperate need of a family situation. He was entirely gang oriented and constantly caused problems for the court and everyone else involved in his case. But since the youth had joined the Umoja family, he had not presented any unmanageable difficulties. The probation officer was amazed and voiced high praise for Umoja.

As the story of its success spread through the grapevine, Umoja also became valuable to the courts. When a youth from Umoja had to appear in court, a Umoja staff member would also attend and stand up for him. Soon the judges began to take notice of the house, and probation officers began recommending the House of Umoja as an alternative to an institution for some youngsters, or as a transition between release from an institution and reentry into the community. Unfortunately, the probation officers, though acclaiming the efforts of the house, neglected to ask if Umoja could financially handle the new referrals from the courts; nor did they indicate that money was available from the state foster care plan. Sister Fattah and the young men, who knew nothing of the foster care plan, accepted the court referrals and continued their limited fund-raising efforts, trying to keep themselves and their newest members afloat.

In 1972 the Youth Development Center of the Pennsylvania Department of Public Welfare decided to set up a group home in Philadelphia. When it was discovered that the House of Umoja had been active for almost four years, the Department of Public Welfare offered to fund it. But the brothers were reluctant and called a special session to discuss the state's offer. They voiced disapproval of the state's bureaucracy and questioned whether Umoja and the state could venture together in a mutual effort. They particularly feared the idea of a "House of Umoja Reformatory," which is what they envisioned if the state were to impose its values and beliefs on the house. After a long, heated debate, the brothers agreed to the merger only after they had been assured that the state would not interfere with the internal procedures of Umoja. This was mutually satisfactory, and the state made the House of Umoja its first group home for delinquents.

A proposal was drawn up between the House of Umoja and the Pennsylvania State Department of Public Welfare. The contract was signed for fifteen of the thirty places Umoja had become accustomed to filling. The other places were kept for emergency placement for boys who were orphaned, deprived, evicted, and the like, who were referred by word of mouth or from other agencies. The state agreed to help renovate a unit that would house the youngsters they were sending. A local television channel in Philadelphia, Channel 10, WCAV, paid for the renovation of the kitchen. Through television and radio editorials and public service announcements, the House of Umoja became a household word.

The objections to the Umoja–state partnership proved to be more prophetic than paranoid as the need to conform to bureaucratic demands in compliance with the contract nearly tore the Umoja program asunder. Other city agencies, a private psychiatric hospital, and a prison for hard-core youths came with offers of contracts for Umoja to accept their more difficult cases; the juvenile prisons used the house as a community reentry point—and suddenly things began to change.

With money came differential pay scales and a regular forty-hour workweek. Umoja residents could not understand why, if all were members of a family and therefore equally favored and equally responsible, it was necessary to pay some more than others. They were hard pressed to understand why cars previously used jointly by all family members for both work and pleasure were now prohibited to members of the family under the age of twenty-five. Was the log that must be kept showing the destination and purpose of the auto trip an indication of distrust? These and other issues created minor antagonisms and resentments that culminated in a major division. As a result, one of the key members of the original fifteen left the House of Umoja, disillusioned and in despair.[6]

Other bouts with the bureaucracy continued to strain and diminish creative initiatives. While the state welfare officials promised no undue interference with Umoja's operation, actions by many state officials betrayed these promises. The first state evaluation claimed that David Fattah's contribution was not essential to the overall performance of the Umoja program and recommended that his position be eliminated. David, who is the father of the House, spends most of his time in the streets helping to resolve gang disputes and negotiating settlements in response to crisis situations. In addition to similar comments on the functions of other personnel, the state raised questions about Umoja's board of directors, which is made up of the Fattahs and their six sons. The state contended that the board of directors should be broadened to include other segments of the community to ensure "accountability." The state also believed that restricting the board of directors to blood relatives was an attempt on the part of the Fattahs to exercise control over the course and direction of the program.

The state contracted with Umoja to assist youngsters who could not be reached through its elaborate array of traditional social work programs and who were not responsive to psychiatric treatment. The state also acknowledged that the Umoja program was effective in altering the behavior of youngsters in their charge—youngsters whom the traditional social work system considered "untreatable." But at the same time, the state evaluators challenged Umoja's structure and style and recommended the addition of professionally trained mental health personnel.

Social workers and criminal practitioners converged on the house seeking information and insight into the methods and techniques that appeared to reach youngsters they found impossible to influence. The Fattahs received numerous requests to give lectures at local colleges and universities. Students from these same institutions came in droves to visit the house to gain some firsthand exposure to the Umoja success. The sudden influx of these visitors began to disturb the order and flow of life within the Umoja program. After a full discussion at a family meeting, it was decided that too much time was being devoted to the new visitors, and therefore severe limits were placed on visitors and speaking engagements.

Another factor that dampened Umoja's enthusiasm for its new-found popularity was the soaring number of gang deaths in the city of Philadelphia. To address this larger problem, the group decided that the spirt of "Imani" (the Swahili word for peace) must reach those outside Umoja if the family were to be true to the fifth principle of Umoja: "Unity within the black community." To achieve this end, a citywide gang conference was planned to bring the gangs together and facilitate their talking with one another.

When first approached about bringing together large numbers of warring gang members for a conference, many young people expressed a reluctance to cooperate, disbelieving that long-standing differences could be resolved in any way other than with a gun. To gain their support, members of the Umoja family appealed in person to gang leaders in prison throughout the state of Pennsylvania. The incarcerated gang leaders provided letters for the Umoja staff to take back to the street leaders who were reluctant to cooperate. These young people were not alone in their apprehension about the conference, as the Umoja family soon discovered when they sought to secure a facility in which to hold the meeting. No place could be found. Civic and religious leaders were fearful of potential damage, since most of the young people had never been in the same room with a rival gang member without the eruption of violence. Finally, representatives of the Philadelphia Society of Friends (Quakers) offered their historic meetinghouse as the site of the gang conference.

Opinion was likewise divided within the Umoja family. David Fattah agreed with many people familiar with gang life that the patterns established by generations of fear, suspicion, and confrontation would never be broken at such a meeting. The consensus of the Umoja family prevailed, however, and the conference planning went ahead. Despite his doubts and uncertainties, David acceded to the will of other members of the family.

Members of Umoja sought the cooperation of the Philadelphia Police Department, requesting that members of the Black Patrol Officers Association assist in providing security for the conference. City Hall refused. The gang conference was to take place on January 1, the same day as the traditional Mummers Parade, but the parade was canceled, and the police were put on alert for the violence expected to erupt with the convocation of so many youth gang members. Tensions were also high among the older Umoja youths who undertook to provide security for the event. Their duties included, among other things, checking and properly labeling guns and other weapons normally carried by gang members when venturing into foreign turfs.

The table for the conference was arranged in circular fashion, similar to that of the United Nations, and the occasion was similarly historic. It marked the first time that most of the gang members had ever been in the same room with one another to resolve an issue without bloodshed. The Fattahs opened the meeting, explaining its purpose and expected outcomes. Falaka's theme was recurrent: "If blacks do not respect the lives of other black people, how can they expect others to respect them?" The conference lasted for five hours with only one disruption. One of the largest gangs in the city disagreed with a traditional rival gang, and they began fighting. The disturbance was quickly quelled by the young men of Umoja, who separated the combatants. When tempers cooled, the meeting resumed, with outcomes that exceeded all expectations.

The gangs agreed on a temporary moratorium on gang fighting. The new council members agreed that one of their first official acts would be to raise money to replace or repair all the furniture that had been broken during the meeting. When the money was eventually collected and presented to the Society of Friends, the Quakers refused, explaining that the furniture was a small price to pay for accomplishments realized in the interest of peace. Many groups signed Imani pacts, promising not to fight other gangs. A United Nations council of gang members was organized to resolve their ongoing differences and to channel employment opportunities. One of the first joint undertakings of the new federation was the printing and sale of tee shirts with the picture of Falaka Fattah inscribed with the word "Imani." The wearing of these tee shirts gave street recognition to youths participating in the truce, and thus they were granted safe passage anywhere in the city. Revenues from the sale of these shirts were used to support other activities of the group.

The Fattahs went on the local radio station that was popular with youth gang members. "Life-a-thons" were broadcast around the clock telling about the conference and asking youths to call in and join in the peace. The response was overwhelming. During the first two months of the peace pact, there was not a single gang-related death in Philadelphia, although previously three was the monthly average.

The Fattah family and the youths that composed the extended family group were not content with addressing the needs of the youth of Philadelphia alone, but reached out to other cities as well. They decided to hold a Black Youth Olympics. In 1976 a delegation from the House of Umoja arranged for youths from Philadelphia to compete with their counterparts in Boston. Two days of athletic events were held in Boston, and the final two days of competition were held in Philadelphia. These events culminated in a banquet at which various medals were awarded to the winners. Over a thousand parents from both Philadelphia and Boston came to the sports events and to the banquet. For some of these parents, it was the first time they had a chance to appear on behalf of their children for positive purposes. For many of the young people, the Black Youth Olympics afforded them the first opportunity to travel out of their cities and to share experiences with others who shared a common plight. In 1977 the olympic games were extended to more than eight cities throughout the country, earning Umoja commendations from two state legislatures.

The Fattahs are catalysts for life, whose commitment to the integrity of the program extends beyond the tenure of any grant. The program was not conceived in response to the availability of any categorical funding, and it will not cease to exist if present funds are withdrawn. In the words of Sister Fattah, "We were caring for young people in residence for three years before the state told us we could receive financial support for what we were doing."

Umoja recognizes that blacks are experiencing the greatest crisis since slavery. The Fattahs do not wait for the effect of the popular notion that jobs, improved education, and housing alone will satisfy the needs of young people. Umoja teaches youths to stand on their own feet despite histories of dependency on and neglect by the larger society. In addition to job-training programs, Umoja's youth are taught to value life—their own and others—and that no adverse social condition justifies the taking of a human life. Self-discipline and a strict adherence to the seven principles is emphasized.

The Umoja program is constantly evolving, altering its activities and style to accommodate the changing needs and tastes of each new group that comes through. In summary, Umoja has been successful in tackling one of the most perplexing problems facing the American public—the behavior patterns of violent youth.

REFERENCES

1. Report by the Department of Public Health, City of Philadelphia, June 1973.
2. Philadelphia Police Department, Crime Report, July 1978.
3. Interview with Sister Falaka Fattah conducted by Diane Palm, research assistant to Robert Woodson, June 2, 1978.
4. David Fattah, interviews with 300 young people, August-September 1969.

5. A nun from the parish explained that although the Catholic church had wanted to help the needy in the black community, it had been reluctant to enter the area. This was in the late 1960s, when the inner city ghettos across the nation were still in flames, so that many social service volunteer groups hesitated to work there, fearing the attitudes and climate of the times.

6. For a year, this young man remained away from the family, working in an automobile factory at a good wage and living the "good life," which included an apartment of his own, new clothes, and a car. Despite his new prosperity, the young man felt a void in his life. Then, in his words, he "OD'ed" (in the figurative sense that he had an overdose of independent living). At age nineteen, the youth returned to the House of Umoja. Falaka and David Fattah were the only parents he had known.

4 AN ANALYSIS OF THE UMOJA MODEL

In November 1973, while millions of Americans watched and listened each evening to television and radio reports of the latest battles and their attendant casualties in the war in Southeast Asia, in Philadelphia, Pennsylvania, the death toll of black male youths resulting from gang violence had climbed to nearly forty for the year. In this same year the leading cause of death for black males between the ages of fifteen and nineteen in the City of Brotherly Love was homicide—10 for every 100,000 black residents.[1] The victims were by no means limited to gang-affiliated youth. In 1972, for example, there were at least seven homicides of persons having no gang affiliation.[2] One person who had cause to worry was Lateef Fattah, who had to survive on the streets of North Philadelphia without the protection of a gang. He recalls his fears: "It was just as bad, not being from a corner, cause when you have no backup out on the streets it's like you're open game, because people don't have to fear repercussions."

While thousands of Americans were actively protesting and organizing to influence the president and Congress to end the war in Vietnam, the Fattah family was working to end the gang wars in Philadelphia. In this chapter I examine how the House of Umoja, serving as a mediating institution and operating independently of the social welfare bureaucracy, has been successful in rehabilitating delinquent and criminally oriented youth. I identify and discuss some of

65

the characteristics critical to the success of Umoja and other self-help and indigenous youth development organizations throughout the country. Since these successes have generated interest from the welfare establishment, I also explore some of the issues associated with the growing demands on Umoja from the public welfare system and the new interest of private businesses and the implications of these new external relations for the continued success of Umoja.

Information on the workings of the House of Umoja was secured through a three-year study of the program. Taped interviews were conducted with thirty former and present Umoja residents in an attempt to record the youths' own accounts of their experiences.[3] Interviews were also conducted, taped and not taped, with Sister Falaka Fattah, founder and director of Umoja, program staff members, and court and welfare referral agents. Data were also obtained from police records.

Half the young men in this sample of thirty were active members of the original Clymer Street gang. The remaining fifteen men represent a broader cross section of youths who lived at the house between 1971 and 1978. They found their way to the house on their own or as referrals from juvenile homes and other welfare institutions that had categorized them as too difficult to help. These young men have extensive histories of contact with the law, mostly through gang-related activities or long-term contact with the social welfare system because of family disruptions or severe emotional problems. Most of the group have actually participated in gang warfare with weapons, have been injured themselves, or have witnessed gang slayings.

The majority of the sample, in or approaching their mid-twenties, still reside in the South Philadelphia neighborhoods from which they sought refuge nearly a decade ago. Although less than half are married, more than half are fathers. Only one of the fifteen has served time in prison for any serious offense since joining the House of Umoja. The fifteen were primarily employed as laborers, machinists, community workers, or retail salesmen. A few had acquired some college or post–high school training. Although life has been fairly normal for these young men since they joined Umoja, most intimated that surviving these years in a city as tough as Philadelphia had been made easier for them by their experiences with Umoja. All take enormous pride in their affiliation with the House.

How has the House of Umoja in ten years successfully transformed more than 500 frightened, frustrated, and alienated young minority males into self-assured, competent, concerned, and productive citizens? After careful observation, study, and participation with the house over the past decade, I have been able to identify very specific ingredients in the operation of Umoja that contribute to its success in turning violent young gang members into responsible, caring, nonviolent citizens; some have developed into active and respected community leaders. The characteristics can be found in some form and varying degrees in similar indigenous efforts serving young delinquents throughout the country (see Chapter 5). It is therefore possible to relate them to the success of these program models in helping talented youths become productive adults.

At least eight characteristics associated with success can be identified in the overall operations of Umoja. They are an inherent part of an ideology, a set of values and principles that have effectively modified the perceptions and behavior of more than 500 young, minority males from some of Philadelphia's most economically deprived communities. All these elements can be identified through observation of the Umoja operation and through study of its policies and practices. They complement one another and often vary in form and degree, but they are an integral part of the overall Umoja approach and merit some enumeration and discussion here. The list includes:

• A family-type organization that is the primary human support system and is based on a participatory model of decision making;
• A process of socialization in which individuals acquire a strong, often new and healthy identity and may even earn the new name of Fattah;
• The Adella, a mechanism for problem solving, that requires full participation of all members;
• Individual learning to organize personal time and space;
• An emphasis on the importance of work, but a redefinition of the meaning of work to associate it with virtue;
• Service to others;
• A spiritual or ideological context expressed in ritual;
• Leadership training and development.

This list is by no means exhaustive. With more study and analysis, one might well identify even more important characteristics embedded in the daily principles and practices of this effective self-help effort.

UMOJA AS A FAMILY MODEL

Membership in the family provides a basic framework for living for all participants at the House of Umoja. Umoja activities are structured to offer a variety of opportunities for black male adolescents to acquire and practice family and community living skills as a normal process of reaching adulthood. In fact, the house was defined by one Philadelphia social worker as "a black family training program."

At the core of the Umoja program is a deliberate grouping around symbols of family. As members of natural families share a social identity and a common socioeconomic "fate," so do the members of the Umoja family. All are inhabitants of an inner city area and are familiar with the same conditions of poverty and unemployment and with the pathologies of social disorganization that these engender. The problems of growing up and getting on in this area are grasped not theoretically, but as living realities. Youths and adults have much in common and readily find they can identify with one another as "family."

The decision to join the Umoja family usually rests with the young person himself, obviating the psychological resistance that accompanies forced association. Youths seeking the sanctuary of unforced, continuous, intimate association present themselves and are voluntarily drawn into the family, its activities, and, incidentally, its personal constraints.

The authority exercised in the group is not that of an outsider with institutional backing and an instrumental commitment to a subordinate; rather, it is the authority of parents over their own children, or that of leadership in close mutual cooperation with an extended family of related adults. Those who enter the program are usually newcomers to responsibility, as are children in a natural family, but they have the routine experience (as children do) of becoming more responsible with the encouragement of family life.

The impact of Umoja's family environment on the youths was repeatedly expressed by them during interviews. This concept of the extended family is believed by the residents and staff of Umoja to be a more direct, human, and possibly more natural solution to the kinds of problems presented by its residents. Roshun Fattah, a Clymer Street gang original and now a street gang worker for a city-funded program, talked about the sense of family at Umoja:

The concept of extended family is the concept that was taught to young people who came here and the concept that is still taught. While black people have lived in America and have developed personal kinds of family relationships, we still, in many instances, have the extended family kind of situations . . . so we kind of capitalized on that to sort of make everyone feel comfortable and to enable everyone to participate in overall activities. . . . This activity is not just for one person, but it's for our family. . . . So we kind of carried ourselves that way, that each person was a member of this intricate family, and Sister Falaka, "Mom," as we call her, and brother Dave was mother and father and the rest of us were like sons.

An interview with William Howard "Skip" Brown revealed that the house organization was structured like an African family, "where everybody got along with everybody." Skip mentioned that he had never experienced that type of environment with his biological family, and he learned something about family structure from Umoja. Other interviews revealed that regardless of the attitude one brought to the house, after the initial adjustment period the House of Umoja became home—and, for some, the first real home.

The experience of Tyrone "Flash" Rockmore illustrates the strong impact the house family had on him. At age fourteen, Flash had spent six months in jail before coming to the house in 1973. Speaking from the perspective of a hard-working grocery store clerk with ambitions of one day becoming a psychologist, he compared Umoja with his previous jail experiences:

They mixed me up with so many different influences that influenced me more as soon as I got back out there [the streets] to jump into something else bad. They placed me at the house—gave me a little freedom, a little bit of pleasure to be out in society instead of barred from society. . . . You can get back out on the streets and do something to clear up that mistake.

Like many others, Flash stayed beyond his discharge period. In fact, he remained at the house for nearly five years, and the only reason he is not seen more regularly by the Fattah family is that he works seven days a week. Reflecting on the impact Umoja had on his life, Flash recalled:

The thing I usually look back on is, if I hadn't went to the House of Umoja, I probably would have kept finding myself going through jail. But it stopped it there because the fact that you had people like Sister Falaka, and her husband, Dave, and their family, plus the brothers and sisters from the House of Umoja as a family . . . everybody cared.

The extended family system at Umoja is a primary supportive system for residents in setting goals. Experiences at the house have moved the young men from looking for a fight or rumble each day to desiring to go to college or choosing careers in community service. Commenting on the important role his peers played in helping him reach some constructive behavioral goals, Lateef recalls that it would have been more difficult going it alone:

> But you see, anytime you tryin' to break away from any kind of peer society, you doing it alone; you feel sort of freakish, you know, like, "Is this really cool?" But if you have a consensus of people from somewhat of the same background—you all live in the city, you all had the same problems, ups and downs, family and all that—it's just a matter of us setting our goals together and motivating and getting what we want.

In short, the family organization at Umoja engages its youth in planning, decision making, and activities related to the survival of the family and overall development of the neighborhood and community in which they live. These activities enable the youths to feel and use their own strengths, to have control over their own lives, and to gain a new kind of faith in themselves and their lives.

Because the family structure offers continuous support for personal needs, Umoja is experienced as an association of true equals, with respect for all, especially for those of the house and family. The past of members is not forgotten or misrepresented as better or worse than it was, but it is not allowed to determine status or future behavior. Communication within the house is not limited or selected by bureaucratic or theoretical considerations external to the person-centered action. Relations are therefore open, voluntary, and fully reciprocal, promoting the chance of unfeigned, personally satisfying commitment to group standards and expectations—a prerequisite for personal change.

DEVELOPMENT OF A NEW IDENTITY

A major reason for the success of Umoja has been the ability of its participants to gauge accurately the state of identity development of its members and to implement appropriate responses. The Umoja experience helps troubled young men acquire a new, healthy identity through membership in the family and, even more, through the opportunity to work toward acquisition of the name Fattah.

Umoja does not seek to reduce delinquency by breaking the bonds of gang cohesiveness. Rather it maintains needed affective relationships between members (often drawing gangs in together) while transforming the terms on which these youths relate to and associate with each other. Gangs become "brothers" in a family in which identities can be elaborated in new directions. Rather than the resocialization of the delinquent, which seeks a relatively quick and dramatic replacement of one socialized pattern by another, there occurs a continuing socialization, which builds on positive aspects of an existing self and calls out new functional adaptations. Encountering one's self and one's community through the ideals and identity signs given in Umoja becomes an act of inward self-transcendence, the elusive objective of rehabilitation programs everywhere.

At the heart of this positive self-change appears the very significant social process of "naming." Perhaps unwittingly the program has hit upon a social-psychological device of great effectiveness. Families always have the privilege of calling their members what they will, and those who enter the Umoja family are likewise renamed. Sometimes, where appropriate, symbols of African origin are selected that carry powerful associations of self-respect. The rhetoric of new labels and symbols rallies new Umojans to organize perceptions of one another and to establish distinctions recognized in their world. Giving and taking a name is a vital signal to the consciousness of the named and of namers alike that a particular character is *there.* A name is an identity of self to oneself and to others. A new name is a new identity with new possibilities for being and relating. Professionals have often noted the self-deforming effects of pejorative labeling of clients in the "degradation ceremonies" of the criminal justice process.[4] In programs such as Umoja this same fundamental principle is at work but in a reverse direction, as the group donation of a positive new name summons a new character in a family member. In fact, a challenging new approach to juvenile justice may have been discovered—the "naming approach" to personal change and neighborhood revitalization.

In contrast, psychiatrically and psychologically oriented groups programmatically undermine and discredit a "bad" self in the effort to promote the individual's acceptance of a "new, improved" self, one the therapist has in mind. The dynamism of the therapist or the pressure of his guided group must overcome the resistance of the "subject."[5]

Jerome Miller, in criticizing existing programs designed for delinquents, calls attention in particular to the implications of authoritarian structures in person-changing groups.[6] He argues that it is necessary to build up the capacity for "authentic listening" if we are truly to understand the clients of these programs and what we are doing to them. All bureaucracies that define and treat "outsiders" must be able to incorporate genuine reciprocity of communication between authorities and clients of the program, as an indispensable prerequisite for authentic personal change. Without accountability and responsiveness to others, guidance between unequals becomes mere coercion and defeats its own ends. The youths themselves must be able to influence what is happening to them at all stages of their contact with the system.[7] Umoja programs appear to have achieved this pattern of reciprocity by having adults and children become "parents" and "family members," who consult each other for guiding standards.

Identity crises and poor self-concepts are frequent and consistent problems among the youngsters who enter the house. The content of many interviews highlights this fact. Lateef Fattah, who was amazed at his own conversion from destructive to constructive behavior and thinking, sums up the effectiveness of youth helping youth. He recalls: "When we was out there rapping to them brothers about not gang warring, we had to understand why they was gang warring and why we used to gang war." By urging their peers to stop fighting, they were reminding themselves to do the same.

Umoja is also successful because it provides youths with a reason for changing themselves. Several of those interviewed emphasized that the Umoja experience helped the members begin to believe in themselves. Once a part of the Fattah family, a youth gave up his gang membership—the supreme test of a new identity. Application of new attitudes and behaviors was demonstrated during times of heavy street conflict among rival gangs when house members mediated peace agreements. Having learned and earned self-respect through dealing with each other at the house, they found it easier to respect gang leaders and persuade them to find less destructive means of resolving gang differences than fighting to the death in the streets.

Primarily through the Adella sessions, the youths acquired a new faith in themselves and others. Roshun Fattah described the process:

> We took the seven principles to give us some guts, some structure. And we tried to build in a responsibility mechanism by indicating to people, depending on what they did, what was acceptable and what was not. This is how people began to get their last name, Fattah—when you had demonstrated that you knew how to handle yourself in some responsible way. In addition to that, you were also aware of the situation that black people were in in this country and were trying to make some kind of contribution to change. And that was the commitment that held us together.

Although the House of Umoja has a very specific, almost ritualistic ideology and a discipline based on that ideology, the house differs radically from some of the cults that cropped up in the United States in the late sixties and in the seventies. The members are always totally free to leave the house, and in their daily activities they are never isolated from the larger community or denied opportunity to work and interact in the neighborhood. Umoja is not an isolated commune; it is an extended family within the larger community. In addition, there is no evidence of corporal punishment to enforce discipline in spite of the fact that violence was previously the major means of self-expression for these gang members. Robert "Fat Rob" Allen is one of the more charismatic members of the house. His observations on house policies best make the point about the voluntary nature of living there:

> They [youths entering the house] are so used to living in a hard criminal way, like from being at the Youth Study Center and places like this where you always get locked doors—people always telling you what to do. . . . Here you have freedom of speech, and the doors are never locked. We do have rules that must be followed, like you must be in at 10:00 P.M. on the weekdays, and on weekends you can go home and visit your family.

A South Philadelphia youth, Ernest "Hawk" Harper, who came to the house in 1976 after spending nearly a year in a juvenile holding center, spoke of the negative attitude he had when he first arrived. He felt that most of the young men who came to the house from institutions had poor concepts about themselves and fears about others that led them to project an image of the bad guy. Hawk was quickly convinced of the sincerity of the extended Fattah family when they aided him after he was stabbed, nearly fatally, in his old neighborhood shortly after coming to the house. He recalls the incident:

> This was about twelve or thirteen days after I came here. I had went back home one day; I had knew some of these guys I was gang warring with and they ran up behind me and stabbed me up . . . About the second faces I saw [were members of my new family]. They didn't really know me, but they was there to help me.

One of the tenets of the House of Umoja is that isolation from the community for extended periods makes reentry and readjustment much more difficult. According to one of its referral sources, one of Umoja's most attractive features is that it "tests bad kids in the community, while all that institutionalization shows is institutional adjustment."[8]

One young man who understands this well is José Bonilla. Born in Puerto Rico in 1962, José lived in New York with his father before moving to Philadelphia in 1960. His first contact with the law occurred at the age of thirteen when he was picked up by the police for fighting. By fifteen, José had spent time in at least five juvenile facilities. José's early chronology of delinquent behavior included stealing, gambling, joining gangs, and burglarizing. Caught burglarizing a home at age fifteen, he was sent to the Youth Study Center for six months and went back and forth to court. Then he was sent to another institution, Franklin Village; then to Chestnut Hill; then back to Franklin Village; then to Lakeside. None of these placements prepared José for community living. When asked how Umoja has changed him, José replied:

> Well, for one thing, I don't steal no more. I don't gang war. That's just out of my mind. In fact, I help brothers. . . . I know a little bit more than I did. . . . One thing I did wrong was to quit school. . . . I'm going back in September. . . . I learned how to ease my mind and think a little better before doing things. The House has taken me away from the things I used to do before that were not positive—given me a lot of good skills.

Those interviewed time and again attributed the changes within their thinking and behavior to increased knowledge and awareness of and respect for themselves as human beings and as developing young black men. They learned how to communicate with others more effectively without resorting to physical violence. This was mentioned by one young man as the most important tool for living gained at the house.

THE ADELLA: A MECHANISM
FOR SOLVING PROBLEMS

Through the Adella sessions, Umoja members gain important experience and skills solving their own problems and in helping other people solve theirs—and without resorting to violence. The Adella serves as the primary mechanism for teaching and learning.

Principles of group dynamics are certainly at work in developing the Umoja family life. The Adella method for resolving the strains of group living is paralleled in some degree in other programs similar to Umoja. The Adella is a routine way for family members to consult one another about family events. Through the Adella, overt control is self-imposed by the group. This form of self-government emphasizes the autonomy and dignity of individual members, while it ensures group loyalty to and participation in shared ideals. As problems and experiences are talked out, consensus is continuously developed and made explicit. The group is seen as the main source of help and support for its member-participants, reinforcing the "we" feeling with its persuasive influence over the will of each.

Adella members, however, through the genuine commitment to self-chosen reciprocities, can build identities without denying initiatives or integrity of the self. The participants are not so much subjects as joint coordinators of their own life. Through the Adella sessions, young people who were prone to violent acting out learned how to put feelings into words. This behavioral change was a significant accomplishment since many of the members had learned early to use violence as a means of expression, and this had been the mode of expected and accepted behavior.

Violent behavior is viewed primarily as learned behavior, rather than as an innate psychic dysfunction, and the Adella sessions are used to teach nonviolent communication skills. Held weekly, these are the chief vehicle through which conflicts are resolved, disputes settled, and self-punishments selected. Fat Rob explained the Adella as follows:

Adella is when all the brothers meet on the weekend to discuss any complaints that they have about anyone at the house. And we have rules, like if anyone has any complaints about anybody, somebody might have to wash dishes for a week or clean up. . . . And $25 fines were levied if any girls are caught in your room [this amount was the cost of a hotel room] ; a dollar a day if you miss school; an allowance of $10 a week for each weekend, but not given if you don't go to school.

Members sit down and discuss problems. If no verbal solution can be reached, a brother will get some form of punishment—nothing harsh. I think this is good because when I was young, nobody cared enough to punish you when you did something wrong. You just got sent to jail, and if you wasn't hard-core before, you'd turn out being one.

The Adella practices were also used constructively to deal with other groups as on the occasion when Umoja House members were instrumental in organizing and successfully conducting the first all-inclusive conference of Philadelphia gangs. The gangs conferred with one another according to Adella principles. In this and subsequent conferences there was a formal system of negotiation. Participants, seated at a round table, their places marked by an identification card, are allowed to have the floor to voice their concerns or to talk about incidents that have occurred and to explain the reasons for them.

Lateef Fattah described the conferences:

They sat down—people known to hate each other—to talk across the table, because that was the only thing that separated them. What I really found surprising in the rap was that we had people sitting there looking at each other that had been on the battlefield maybe a month ago or less trying to take each out of here. Representatives from gangs like the Valley and Norris Street have been fighting each other so long that some of the people gang warring don't know how it all got started.

The conferences have had a positive effect on other gangs, which began to view Umoja as an important and viable community institution to be respected. They also changed many individual gang leaders. The present job counselor at Umoja recalls that he had not made a commitment to stop gang warring until he was persuaded to attend a 1972 Umoja-sponsored conference. The recognition and respect given to all those in attendance created an environment in which Umoja's message of peace was well received.

The Adella sessions also bring out the natural creative potential in many of the members. For example, one leading house member began working with three gangs in West Philadelphia that had all fought each other. As a result of his efforts, they began working together and formed a council of members from the rival gangs. The council inspired Fat Rob to write a play about gang life that was performed at a local school before an audience of a thousand

and was dedicated to Sister Fattah. The young playwright credited Sister Fattah and Umoja with his personal development and success and stated that "if it wasn't for Sister Fattah and others like her, I probably would have ended up dead or in jail permanently."

Although the Adella as structured at the House of Umoja probably could not be replicated by an unconnected group in another community, it represents the key to socializing youths and molding their behavior in more positive forms. The Adella is not a substitute for the family but an authority within the family system where decisions are made. Decision-making responsibility does not lie with one person, such as a patriarchal or matriarchal figure, but is decentralized through the Adella mechanism. The Adella also provides further evidence that the charismatic quality of Sister Fattah is not the only moving force or determinant of success at Umoja. Rather, emphasis is placed on dialogue, peer accountability, and cooperative planning. Principally through the Adella and other group and family meetings, youths learn how to express themselves in an encouraging environment and in front of people they have grown to trust. As one of those interviewed put it: "The importance of this communication tool often makes the difference between life and death out on the streets."

LEARNING TO ORGANIZE TIME AND SPACE

The house operates on time schedules and systems for managing daily living; thus, all members learn to adopt and adjust to behavior that requires the organization of space and time. Before coming to Umoja, most of the young men have not managed this aspect of their lives well. In fact, having "time on their hands," being unemployed and bored, with nothing to do, are conditions that often precipitate delinquent and criminal behavior.

The house teaches the importance of time, respect for space and individual privacy, and the need for planning in one's life. This instruction is crucial in transforming antisocial behavior into acceptable behavior. This realization came forcefully to many of Umoja's young members, and Robert's story tells it best.

Slight in stature for his sixteen years, Robert Selby represents the house at various community meetings, conferences, and other public events. His main love, however, is helping other youths like himself rid themselves of destructive behavior patterns. His credentials for "dealing with the brothers' heads," as he puts it, are simply the experiences that led him to Umoja.

"RS" is no stranger to violence. As a seven-year-old he witnessed a "brother get his head shot off" in his South Philadelphia neighborhood. This occurred at the time the Fattahs were opening up their home to those attempting to escape gang violence. Because of his parents' separation and mother's illness, RS moved frequently from one household to another within his biological extended family, living in turn with his mother, his grandmother, an aunt, and his father. He openly admits that his temper caused problems with his father, which eventually landed him in Southern Homes for Children, a placement for emotionally disturbed youths, where he spent sixteen months before coming to the House of Umoja.

Robert described his first months at Umoja and the factors that contributed to his conversion:

> Well, when I first got here, the counselors wouldn't let me do what I wanted to do. They stayed on by butt. "You going do what you supposed to do." I guess I needed somebody to do that to me. . . . I hate when people criticize me, and they all knew that so they all criticized me. . . . So like I said to myself one day, I'm just going to grow up and be like everybody else.

Pressure to use his time better and perform specific assigned tasks led him to set some personal and educational goals for himself. Since his temper had caused a rift with his father, one of his major personal goals was a reconciliation. Robert feels that the Umoja experience has helped him to face his limitations and shortcomings, which is helping him and his father heal an afflicted relationship. Robert's other goal is to go home with a job. He proudly asserts that he wants not to be a burden, but to have something to offer. Knowing he has to graduate from high school before being able to take on a full-time job, Robert is determined to complete his education. Having learned how to work toward goals, his long-range ambition is to build his own home some day.

WORK AS SERVICE TO OTHERS

Service to others is upheld as a basic principle of living, and the opportunity to provide service is central to the daily activities at Umoja.

In addition, service carries with it high status and is viewed as an important human responsibility, in no way associated with servility. This concept simply stated is "Those who help are helped the most."[9] Giving service to others is also a fundamental ingredient in most self-help approaches, and because of its emphasis in Umoja activities the house program is seen as a brand of self-help.

Amazingly, youths who were hostile toward others, self-centered, and who never offered to assist others before coming to Umoja are now expressing concerns about their brothers and others in the community and reporting on their personal enjoyment in giving service. At Umoja giving service has been incorporated in the concept of work. Besides working in the community attempting to stop gang warfare, residents are expected to do domestic chores as a means of learning the importance of work, developing good work habits and a sense of responsibility, and contributing to the overall maintenance of the family. The survival of Umoja's extended family depends on the willingness of its able-bodied members to work at whatever is necessary and available. These experiences are seen as crucial to the development of self-reliance and self-discipline.

For Umoja youths the social dependency fostered by years with the welfare system has hindered development of the self-discipline needed to acquire and maintain employment. In addition, they have grown up as members of a minority in an urban area denied real work opportunities. Thus the burden falls on the family at Umoja to develop meaningful work for its members.

It was always with great pride that present and former residents talked of their job or work at the house. Regardless of assignment, no task was seen as menial; each contribution was seen as essential to the overall development and maintenance of the program and the family. Those whose work was primarily janitorial talked with the same kind of pride about what they did as those who were assigned to the more prestigious security force. Whatever their work, it was approached with a philosophy of service. Sixteen-year-old Darryl Douglas described himself as being very lazy when first arriving at the house. Only seven months later, he proudly informed visitors that his job was to help keep the buildings clean.

With an official unemployment rate of 45 percent among black youths in Philadelphia and an unofficial rate estimated at 60 percent, finding good jobs is especially difficult for Fat Rob and others who work as employment counselors. The attitude of youths seeking work and the possible negative consequences of failure were described by Jusari Fattah, the eldest of Falaka and Dave's six biological sons:

> All the brothers that are involved in our employment program now are former gang members. We're now trying to get them situated into a nice job. . . . Some of them want to go back to school and finish up their education, and we're helping them out in whatever way we can. But the main thing we've focused on is trying to get them jobs because that creates a lot of problems. If they don't have any money—then what else can they do? They are trying to avoid robberies. You know the only reason why they do that is because they don't have any funds. A lot of them have kids that they would like to support, and it's really hard for a male when he can't provide for his family, so a lot of them are forced in a situation of robbery and burglary.
>
> I think a lot of them are interested in work and they really would like to work if they could find a job. . . . I learned that from the brothers that we're working with now. They come to work on time and they really want to work. They'd rather do something so they can have some money in their pocket. A lot of them have served, and they realize being incarcerated is not really helping their situation. It takes a whole lot away from a person, being incarcerated.

Fat Rob described the dedication and commitment of those who often find themselves working at the house without pay because of a lack of funds:

> There's just so many things they got to offer here, and the unique thing about it is it's been done a long time without any funds at all. When people are not paid to do a service, most of the time, they give up. But here, sometime we don't get paid for three, six months, maybe a year sometime, but we all stay here and give to each other. If this person's working, then that person he'll give. I think the brothers, they learn self-respect here. When they leave here, they'll know how to go and get their own place and take care of themselves, and then again, when all the brothers leave here—in a way, they never leave cause they always coming back, pitchin' in, giving a hand.

Umoja's redefinition of work is in sharp contrast to the traditional concept of one man of lesser status and authority working for another. For house members, helping others means helping themselves, and they work collectively to address the needs of the family and the larger community. Integrated with the concept of service is a host of needs, such as protecting the neighborhood against crime and vandalism, caring for children, repairing houses, and assisting in providing recreational opportunities for youngsters. In return for labor a youth receives clothing, food, temporary shelter, and other forms of acknowledgment. There is less emphasis on individual pursuits than on collective goals and achievement. These measures of success are not always understood or given credence by the professional human service agencies. Although Umoja shares many values with the larger community, it has also evolved a unique set of values rooted strongly in the African heritage. These beliefs have been translated into the concepts of service and work as practiced by Umoja members.

A SPIRITUAL CONTEXT

The House of Umoja teaches ethics and provides its members a spiritual context primarily through activities based on religious attitudes, beliefs, and practices expressed in the Adella sessions. Initially, Sister Fattah taught the meaning and significance of a life; then the older members passed it on to newcomers. Fat Rob cited his personal conversion:

> The main thing that made me stop gang warring and made me start liking the work of the house was that Sister Fattah explained to all the brothers what a life meant. . . . I didn't really know the meaning of life. It didn't really mean nothing to me to go out there and fight the other brothers and see one of them get killed or hurt or something like that. It was something I felt I had to do. Sister Fattah sat down and explained. It's just something, she said, that a person is a human being. A life is a valuable thing that you have.

Through the Adella, the cultural heritage, rituals, and folklore of Africa are taught. Through information about their African past and the history of their people's struggles for survival in this country, the youths begin to develop respect for themselves, their families, and others. The discovery that their class and race of people have a proud history, opened new horizons for these youths, who had little or no hope for a different kind of life before joining Umoja.

LEADERSHIP TRAINING

Leadership qualities in individual members are identified, supported, and developed at Umoja. Teachings, practices, and reward systems provide a variety of opportunities for leadership. Some observers may be tempted to attribute Umoja's success entirely to the charismatic qualities of Sister Fattah—a strong, almost mystical matriarchal figure. Sister Fattah attributes her own qualities and capabilities to her exposure to charismatic adults during her childhood and early adulthood. She points out that leadership models abound in the neighborhoods of Philadelphia. This rich resource of human capital can be tapped to deal with social problems such as juvenile delinquency if community-based mediating structures are supported more.

After three years of study and an even longer period of observation and friendly association with the House of Umoja, I am convinced that the House is a viable institution. With adequate financial resources and public support, it can endure for generations to come and accommodate the new leaders who are destined to succeed Sister Fattah.

The annual conferences of gang members, the council of gangs, which has sponsored special cultural and recreational events, the play portraying the gang problem, and the speeches to professional and civic groups on the work of the house—all demonstrate the ability of the young leaders developed and nurtured at Umoja. Members of the house who were once gang leaders, including Brother David Fattah himself, have rechanneled their talents into more positive endeavors.

PROBLEMS WITH THE BUREAUCRACIES

As noted previously, Umoja operated for several years with little or no financial assistance from the state or local governments, but as its reputation grew, the courts, probation departments, and protective service agencies recognized that among the young men sheltered by the Fattah family, attitudes and behavior were significantly improved and had fewer contacts with the law enforcement agencies.

One youth, who had been sent to a mental institution as a placement of last resort, was told by his social worker that his release was contingent upon finding a suitable foster placement, but his history of violent and aggressive behavior made it difficult, if not impossible, for the agency to find anyone willing to accept him. The youth found Umoja on his own. When the social worker visited the House of Umoja to conduct the customary home evaluation, she was awed by what she discovered. From then on, the agency used Umoja as a group home for hard-to-place young men, although these initial placements were made informally. Umoja's effectiveness was demonstrated when the boys sent there were no longer problems for the agencies and courts. Some members of the agency then sought to obtain a purchase-of-service contract for Umoja as a foster group home. Informal recognition, however, proved to be much easier to obtain than an official contract for the appropriation and expenditure of state funds.

One state official in charge of services to youth voiced what many others believed strongly—that the Umoja program was being exploited, since it was providing free care for youngsters who would otherwise be on the state's budget. This official advocated establishing Umoja as the first group home in the state of Pennsylvania to serve delinquent youth.

The attempt to secure a services contract from the state generated a great deal of interest in Umoja by politicians, social workers, and others and brought about an entirely new political struggle for Sister Fattah and the House members. For example, when Umoja's application was being processed, members of the Pennsylvania State Assembly subjected it to a more intensive review than other applications from the traditional social welfare agencies. Many assembly members and agency bureaucrats were reluctant to fund an indigenous organization with a name they found difficult to pronounce. Questions were raised about Umoja's teaching of black culture, and the house was accused of teaching racial preference. Argument after argument was thrown in the path of a smooth negotiation of a services contract to Umoja. Its indigenous nature and overwhelming success were unknowns that threatened the state's politicians and welfare power structure.

The fears and ambivalence about engaging in a contractual relationship were not confined to the state officials. The youths who had helped build Umoja and their local community supporters voiced strong reservations about accepting state assistance, as we have already noted. Many viewed welfare services as an appendage of an oppressive child welfare system. They feared that Umoja would become a mere extension of the welfare bureaucracy, turning into a "jail rather than a home." The issue of state intervention in the Umoja family was debated long and hotly at Adella sessions.

Many of the young men's fears were substantiated when the state consented to fund Umoja. The state funds did not flow into Umoja freely but carried many strings. Because state welfare funds went to eligible individuals rather than to homes or organizations, the way funds were used was regulated in a way that was disruptive to the participatory system of the House of Umoja. Youngsters who were referred by the social services department were singled out, by contract, as the ones to benefit from the state funds. Despite an atmosphere of shared responsibility and partnership, suddenly some members appeared to be of greater value than others as salary scales were established for the first time.

After several conflicts with the welfare bureaucracy on the insensitive and inappropriate application of its regulations to Umoja, one of the original young residents left in protest, denouncing the family for having compromised its principles. Other members became less responsible and enthusiastic about carrying out work assignments. Much of this was attributed to the fact that they were now being paid with state funds for what used to be considered service to the family. There were also disputes among members over salary scales since, by regulation, some were paid more than others. Another disruption that arose from state intervention was that youths officially referred from the state agency remained wards of the state and could never be "true" family members. As a result, several of them perceived Umoja as just another state-run facility, and they initially expressed no obligation to conform to the principles that governed others at the house.

Several nontraditional social workers assisted Umoja in its negotiations with the child welfare bureaucracy and helped mediate issues between the state and Umoja about the rules and regulations, many of which conflicted or were irrelevant and inappropriate to the successful operation of this extended family model. These advocates within the child welfare system successfully interpreted Umoja's goals and positive impact on the youths it served. State rules and regulations, however, consistently operated at variance with the Umoja approach.

One such rule is Section 7100 of the state's Youth Service Act, which requires each program funded by the state to have on its staff a full-time trained social worker.[10] Umoja consented to a full-time trained social worker to work with the young men, but conflicts surfaced almost immediately after his arrival. His first act was an attempt to organize group therapy sessions, with himself as therapist and group leader. This proposal met with immediate resistance by the Umoja family since the Adella served as the primary vehicle for resolving individual problems or interpersonal differences. In the Adella each person assumed equal status as a human being without any of the labels of the traditional group therapy approach. The Adella won out.

In another instance the social worker attempted to gain confidence and trust from some of the youngsters by suggesting that house rules be changed to increase allowances. He was chided by house leaders and informed that youngsters could receive additional income only if they performed an additional chore. He was also told that this approach reinforces a strong work ethic, which is essential to the building of good character.

Other differences between Umoja and traditional child welfare placements occur in program goals. For example, the courts and youth service bureaus define success as an individual's avoidance of any further police contact even though the youngster may be engaging in other self-destructive activities, such as alcoholism or other consensual offenses. For Umoja, success is determined not only by staying out of trouble with the law, but also by observable changes in attitude and behavior and most of all by the ability to sustain a responsible relationship with a girlfriend, a blood family member, or a wife and child. The contrasts in philosophies between Umoja and the traditional human service system are clearly expressed in a criticism once made by Sister Fattah: "In this society, as long as a man maintains a good work record, he is free to go home and abuse his wife and children as often as he desires."

The conflicts between Umoja and the state bureaucracy caused deep concern among the Fattahs, and the extended family experienced its most severe tests. These conflicts would have destroyed many indigenous groups whose bonds were merely organizational and structural or who were held together primarily to further an individual's career. In Umoja, however, the family structure provided a strong defense against such threats. The conflicts were settled in special Adella sessions where compromises were forged and spiritual bonds reinforced. The house weathered the storm, and Sister Fattah and others working patiently and with the welfare bureaucracy managed to keep the house and state funding intact. To this day, problems continue with the state agency about the limits of its intervention into the operation of the house, but the referrals keep coming and troubled young men are being helped.

Cooperation with the state has also given rise to administrative problems because the allotment of state and federal funds imposes a false economy on programs such as Umoja. First, funds are often restricted to use for certain categories of expenditures, although the needs of the individual are multiple and a program such as Umoja takes a comprehensive approach to service. The funds allocated are therefore less than needed to perform the most adequate job. Second, the money is provided for a limited time, after which the program is expected to secure funding from other sources or become an extension of the local or state government service system. A related problem is that these limited funds are often given as reimbursements, and state money does not always arrive on time. Thus, small community-based programs are forced into many financial maneuvers in which the staff is often not adept and which detract from more crucial program activities.

Funding is the most chronic and menacing problem for indigenous organizations. Their overall operations are conducted in the midst of poverty. Umoja has found a way to help youngsters stay out of trouble and develop into responsible citizens in economically deprived communities like West Philadelphia, but it has not been able to have a significant effect on the economic conditions of its neighborhood. Indigenous programs cannot be expected to perform miracles, and the larger economic problems of many urban communities need to be tackled. We must also examine the policies of government and of private enterprise as they influence or fail to influence the socioeconomic status of communities in which they have varying interests. Umoja can go a long way in rehabilitating individuals and instilling or restoring self-respect in these young men, but it will need the help of direct funding so that the family can be economically viable. Also needed is more planned development to restore and maintain some viability in the community in which the members of the House of Umoja must survive and grow.

Umoja is not a conscious attempt to enact professional social science theory. Instead the program developed from natural efforts of the family to support itself, with all members contributing. Fundraising activities gave the family an important new sense of itself and a way of measuring meaningful progress. Its activities expanded as

Umoja identified and tried to meet specific needs of families and others in the local area, working in the community setting with existing community structures. Finally, Umoja also undertook to proselytize for its way of life. The group family began to help people in trouble "find themselves," so that those who had been helped at Umoja in turn became helpers.

The ideal of service to others reappears in all the community-based programs discussed in the following chapter, providing another very central source of strength for continuing socialization. It has been observed that people who convert others reinforce their own commitment to their animating faith. A basic condition for giving and receiving is that the receiver be in a position to reciprocate the gift. If he is merely a dependent receiver of favors, however well meant by the giver or useful to himself, he will end by despising the gift and rejecting the giver. In the ideal of service to others, Umoja members find it easier to accept what is done for them without loss of self-respect as they in turn begin to help others. Their new goals and values are reinforced as they step into their community to encounter others in another character—in an admired role in a different script. The "changed" become "changers" themselves.

A last point is that the family of Umoja lives at home, not in an alien atmosphere. It is located in the inner city, where criminogenic forces are concentrated, as are the populations that produce the child at risk, who is usually passed over and warehoused by juvenile justice programs. Since massive social restructuring of the economic and material realities of urban centers is beyond the scope of the family, Umoja sets out to change the inner adaptation of its youth to his own neighborhood. In this commitment, the program of Umoja faces two ways, inward toward the person and the needs of the child and outward toward the needs of neighbors. The activities of the House of Umoja are directed to both levels of need, by fostering mutual, reciprocal relations between the community and child of the community. In the end, child saving is also neighborhood revitalization in a profound way.

Other successful community programs for youth provide supportive evidence for this analysis of the House of Umoja. These programs have apparently developed spontaneously and independently of the Philadelphia project; yet in their efforts to deal with the same complex problems, they have organized themselves in ways that closely resemble the social form of Umoja. Descriptions of a few of these neighborhood youth groups in the following chapter will make the point clear.

REFERENCES

1. Data are from the Philadelphia, Pennsylvania, City Health Department, 1973.
2. *Final Report: Evaluation of Youth in Conflict Service Project* (Washington, D.C.: Safe Streets, Inc., March 1974), sec. 2, p. 1.
3. For more on this method, see Clifford R. Shaw, *The Jack Rollers* (Chicago: University of Chicago Press, 1930).
4. Harold Garfinkel, "Conditions for Successful Degradation Ceremonies" *American Journal of Sociology* 61 (January) 1956: 420–4.
5. The ability to interrupt a personality attempting to maintain its own coherence is the test of psychology-based programs.
6. Jerome G. Miller, *The Revolution in Juvenile Justice (From Rhetoric to Rhetoric)* (Gambier, Ohio: Kenyon Public Affairs Forum, 1978), p. 54.
7. Ibid., pp. 53–6.
8. Interview with Robert Ridley, director of community services, Youth Development Center, February 12, 1978.
9. Frank Reissman, "How Does Self-Help Work?" *Social Policy* 7, no. 2 (September/October 1976): 42.
10. State of Pennsylvania, Youth Service Act, Title 7100, Group Home Regulations, June 1969.

5 OTHER PROGRAM MODELS

Juvenile correction programs generally fail to correct very much and deterrence does not deter, while the juvenile justice system neglects the poor, urban, minority youths who account for a disproportionate amount of the most serious crime. Against this background of stubborn facts, general disillusionment, and lack of innovative thinking, the emergence of the House of Umoja is of special interest. Umoja is an alternative resource that continues to change the lives of precisely that youth group marked by professional research as categorically the most dangerous, the most apt to repeat their offenses, and the least amenable to change.

The paradox of the juvenile corrections systems is that a bureaucratically organized, theoretically sophisticated structure of secondary relations is unable to dictate rationally planned action that will engender the primary bonding required for juvenile clients to change themselves. The power of the agency to design and to allocate roles is specific. The abstract knowledge of person formation in primary bonding groups is extensive. But the inability to create wholesome primary relationships through institutional fiat is the "uneven and uncertain" effect of institutional model programs for juveniles that research continually turns up.

If Umoja's approach actually attracts young people and evokes from them new commitments and new self-images through participation in Umoja's groups, it suggests that feelings of kinship or family closeness and support are genuinely tapped.

For the youths participating in this neighborhood group, there is continuous support for a new identity of positive value, while the need for meaningful and exciting activities, formerly met in many cases by the delinquent gang, is now met by the program. In contrast with institutionally sponsored treatments, this local, nonprofessional approach appears able to mediate between the identity needs of the youths and the large-scale institutions of public society in ways not available to outside professionals.

Umoja, a community-engendered and -managed program, may turn out to be precisely the type of innovation that is emphatically called for by professionals. It is fairly easy to point out practical or theoretical objections to current ways of handling delinquents but, naturally, more difficult to demonstrate that new ways are feasible or will in the long run have greater success. Nevertheless, Umoja's program continues to suggest the intriguing possibility that a successful alternative is being worked out. If "nothing works," as Martinson has declared,[1] it is still clear that the results of Umoja are at least as valuable as the doubtful, insignificant, or even negative effects of more professional programs.

The House of Umoja is not unique. Other programs have spontaneously reproduced all or most of its basic features, strongly suggesting that Umoja is not an accidental success or a singular, nonreplicable approach that would fall in the tails of a probability curve. Other dynamic, indigenous inner city programs appear to utilize the same methods for promoting the positive reorientation of their members and with similar success.

Three examples of many such programs beginning or under way are the South Arsenal Neighborhood Development Program (SAND) in Hartford, Connecticut, the Youth-In-Action (YIA) Program in Chester, Pennsylvania, and the La Playa neighborhood program in Ponce, Puerto Rico. Like Umoja, they are actively helping their youths to get out of or stay away from trouble. In each case they are also having an important effect in their communities, bringing out the abilities of local groups, pulling neighbors together, and alerting them to possibilities for dealing with their own problems.

LA PLAYA DE PONCE

La Playa, the port section of Ponce, the second largest city of Puerto Rico, has a population of more than 17,500, or 10 percent of Ponce itself. La Playa has always been a distinctive area, adjacent to but separate from Ponce and notorious as the "bad" section of town, inhabited by "people nobody wants to touch." It was long considered too dangerous to walk through and generally avoided by outsiders. Rates of juvenile delinquency and crime ran twice as high as those of Ponce itself, and politicians had written off La Playa as too problem ridden for effective programs of social reconstruction. Poverty, unemployment, drug addiction, acute lack of social services, and advanced deterioration of the physical and social complex plagued the area. For community children there was nothing to do and no future. Very few were completing school. La Playa itself was made up of twenty small sectors or groups that did not talk to or interact with one another. No medical services were available to combat the extensive effects of poverty, poor nutrition, and unsanitary living conditions. La Playa was a ghetto, very like inner city areas of mainland America.

Since 1968 Sister Isolina Ferré, of the Order of Missionary Servants of the Blessed Trinity, has worked to unite Playeros in self-directed efforts against La Playa's many problems. With five sisters of her order, one social worker, one employee of the Agricultural Extension Agency, and a sewing machine, she began her community and human development program. The Center for Orientation and Services was established in 1968 through community leadership and concerted voluntary efforts generated among these formerly alienated, unorganized area residents. There are now four extensions of the original center in different sectors of La Playa, offering a variety of community services and activities.

Vocational workshops prepare youths for jobs in industry; there are home management workshops for girls, formal tutoring in academic subjects, and many nonacademic activities to help young people discover and develop their skills in horticulture, cosmetology, and in photography, ceramics, and other art forms. In addition, there are many activities oriented to general cultural development—excursions, a sports program, a steel band, a social club with counseling available on social relations and conduct. A little country house (La Casa del Balcon) is open to all and serves as a point of entry into center programs. Here art work and photography from center workshops are displayed, and young people gather to talk and relax. At this conversation center, there is always someone to listen, and young Playeros discover in the course of the talk that they want to do something with their lives.

But recreational and educational services are not the only changes in La Playa. Volunteers from the area now publish a community paper to keep everyone informed about center activities and local events. A Ford Foundation grant has been secured to teach horticulture and to train nurses' aides for the care of old people and babies, meeting important needs in the area. A program for the handicapped and the retarded trains workers in their care and provides supportive counseling for mothers and families of special children to help improve family relations generally. Young people of the center provide many services to older Playeros, helping them with their problems and aiding them to get about La Playa safely. An annual communitywide festival draws everyone together socially to celebrate the achievements of the center as achievements of the people of La Playa themselves, reinforcing the idea that as a group they can in fact find the resources to deal effectively with community problems.

Another program, called *abuelos adoptivos*, or foster grandparents, associates residents aged sixty and over with children and their families who may need the mature skills of these senior companions. The adoptive grandparents can recapture a sense of their own ability to contribute to others' needs, while the adopted ones find a personal relationship that can develop into an important source of support, advice, and satisfaction.

Also developed were regular monthly meetings, well attended and supported, to discuss any topic of special concern to the community. Playeros met to search out one another's ideas, opinions, and complaints concerning the administration of justice in La Playa, the role of the schools, the functioning of public institutions, and the pressures that are changing local norms and customs. The values, culture, and history of La Playa were also discussed. The goal was to increase public knowledge of what was happening in the community—especially to promote critical awareness of how local institutions influence the development of the children and of family unity within the community. These discussions, like all center-sponsored programs, emphasized the values of family life and the identity of Playeros as members of a community family.

With the expansion of center activities, the community began to feel their effects in more and more areas of neighborhood life. A group was formed to act as interagency coordinator, mediating between various local groups and agencies to prevent duplication of services, helping to organize new activities, and improving communication and cooperation generally, especially with the police, the labor department, welfare services, the family court, and other institutions bearing on La Playa's problems.

The establishment of the La Playa health care clinic is one of two very striking achievements of the Center for Orientation and Services. Sister Isolina writes that originally there were no health services in the area. A doctor might come in occasionally, but usually people had to go outside for care. Sister Isolina, working through the Office for Economic Opportunity, was able to have a doctor who was a high official in Washington, D.C., inspect the health situation in La Playa. When he walked through the slums and saw the stagnant green water under houses, he "couldn't believe his eyes." As a result of this visit, a Family Health Comprehensive Services Grant was obtained, but the community itself had to organize and supervise the administration of the health services. Accordingly, Sister Isolina called a general community meeting and told one hundred astonished people assembled there that they could have $1 million for a health care center if they would elect a board of directors and take charge of the project. The result was the establishment of the present Cento de Diagnostico y Tretamiento, a comprehensive family health center created with a community board of directors, composed mostly of people with little or no formal education and elected from a neighborhood that had never before had any community action.

The community reports that at first the government had difficulty accepting the ability of these local people to run such a project. It was even harder for the people themselves to accept it. Yet the medical program has worked for more than five years on a budget exceeding $1 million, giving health service in that time to more than 15,000 people. The place is beautiful, clean, and not vandalized in an area once notorious for the malicious mischief and delinquent activities of its youth. Community people, having learned to run the medical center, have also learned to take pride in this project that belongs distinctively to them. The center is widely regarded as the best family health service in Puerto Rico, drawing officials from all over to study not only the administration of the medical center but also the vital community process that has made this health center possible.

The other very remarkable achievement of community development in La Playa has been the dramatic reduction of youthful crime and delinquency. Without any funding at the beginning and armed only with a philosophical commitment to foster the "unfolding of the human potential in community children,"[2] Sister Isolina began to help young people in trouble with the courts and school dropouts. Among these a hard-core element disproportionately contributed to the police statistics and to the unsavory reputation of La Playa.

The influence Sister Isolina built up with hard-core delinquents was originally not mandated or enforced by the courts, but grounded entirely in the ideals and the concerted efforts of local people who began to conceive of themselves as responsible for community children. Lacking a residence for children, Sister Isolina set about building relations with the young people in trouble and with their families and neighbors. She found that often the schools had refused any further contact with these "bad" children, who were rejected or abandoned by others to "run wild" in the streets. As a counterinfluence, Sister Isolina began to organize alternative education programs, using a small grant from the Law Enforcement Assistance Administration (LEAA) that had to "take care of everything." Many workshops were initiated to provide cultural enrichment, opportunities to learn employable skills, and, most of all, the social milieu that encourages young people to discover and take an interest in their own potential. Delinquents are "renamed" as young adults, as officers of clubs, as artists, skilled technicians, future parents, citizens, and the like; at the same time, adults of the area acquire new identities as advocates *intercesores*, board members, community planners, and activists. It was a policy from the beginning to stress the idea that the equipment and tools of the workshops belong to the children themselves and to their neighbors, not to the staff, thus eliciting a pride in them and an ability to care for things.

Since many of the children lacked the most basic educational achievement, it was necessary to invent a way to cultivate the individual by building on some interest he already had. In La Playa adolescent boys are fascinated with horses and stealing them has the same appeal that stealing cars does in some cities of the United States. By taking advantage of the universal interest in horses, the center was able to attract many young people. Without commenting on the stealing itself or trying to apprehend or punish thieves, the center announced an equestrian club and drew a large number of enthusiastic volunteers, each bringing his "own" (stolen) horse. A veterinarian was recruited to the center to explain how to care for horses and to discuss riding and related topics. This inspired intense discussions that went beyond horses to matters of club organization and to questions of values and personal conduct. When the boys demanded to know how to run meetings, parliamentary law and *Robert's Rules of Order* were explained to them. Officers were elected so that each had to learn the responsibilities pertaining to his office. When the secretary-elect did not know how to read and write, he came around asking to be taught.

Little by little the youths themselves found it necessary to learn things and sought answers to problems. The process of learning was intimately bound up with their own initiative. In the course of a growing involvement of young Playeros with the center activities, horse stealing gradually stopped. At first, says Sister Isolina, people nobody wanted to touch were running wild over the streets with stolen horses, but then these same boys became part of a society organized with recognized rules and values.[3]

Before Sister Isolina began her work, it was considered unsafe to walk in La Playa, at any time of the day or night. Now there is less stealing and less violence among Playeros involved with the center, and no homicide has occurred in La Playa in four years among the juvenile population. The schools continue to report some damage to school property, but there is much less vandalism at the program centers and in the neighborhood itself. La Playa, being a port, was once notorious for the sale and use of hard drugs, but the work of the center appears to have reduced their incidence. Little more than some marijuana and glue are now used among the youths, and few hard drugs are found in the area. Significantly, all categories of juvenile offenses recorded by police show a marked reduction in La Playa since the program has been in effect.

The population of La Playa according to the 1970 census was 15,574, with more than 50 percent less than ten years old. In 1970 the group served by the center, youths between the ages of ten and twenty-five, made up more than one-third of the entire population. Since then, because of the construction of two new urban developments, the youth population has grown considerably.

Police statistics comparing La Playa with adjacent Ponce strongly suggest the positive effect the programs of the center are having in reducing and preventing delinquency (see Table 5-1). Inasmuch as La Playa is one-tenth the size of Ponce, the figures show a disproportionately high rate of juvenile delinquency in the La Playa ghetto. But the figures also show that La Playa is changing. When the incidence of offenses is compared with population totals in both areas, the ratio of offenses is fairly constant in Ponce, while the ratio of La Playa, adjusted to the computed youth population growth in recent years, shows a two-thirds decline since 1968, when Sister Isolina began her center.

The activities of the center promote a progressive involvement of adult groups and youths in services and concern for one another, which has a pervasive effect on the quality of life in La Playa. In addition, the center has established specific ways of working with neighborhood boys in trouble with the police. The juvenile court now sends them "incorrigibles," status offenders, drug addicts, and worse. The center's work with these hard-core cases is conceded to be more successful than the probation supervision that was formerly common. Boys are not merely returned to the streets, but are invited into a network of caring relations and positive activities through which they often develop a changed consciousness of themselves. They come to see the community of La Playa as the scene of their own worth-

Table 5-1.   Juvenile offenses registered for Ponce and La Playa, 1968-77.

Year	Ponce (including La Playa)	La Playa
1968-69	709	133
1969-70	787	120
1970-71	721	85
1971-72	970	99
1972-73	762	81
1973-74	590	79
1974-75	483	54
1975-76	627	89
1976-77	830	114

Source: Estadisticas de la Division de Ayuda Juvenil de Ponce.

while contributions and their own personal growth. As a result, Sister Isolina reports that only six or seven boys a year from La Playa become involved with the courts; in these cases the center's adults (advocates) intercede for them at court. Usually, however, the neighborhood children are stopped before the police pick them up. Members of the community now act as an early warning system, bringing to the center themselves anybody who seems to be headed for trouble. When this happens, an advocate is assigned to the boy to involve him in center programs.

The role of the advocate, or intermediator-educator, is integral to the operation of the center and reflects the capacity of culturally or socially homogeneous neighborhood groups to rally to symbols of kinship and to function together as if they were extended families. The idea of the advocate, like that of adoptive grandparents, is based in community understanding and a shared responsibility that goes beyond the achievement of short-term practical goals. The advocates are young adults who have grown up in the area under the same conditions that contribute to the delinquency of their charges; they know exactly the feelings and problems that confront these youths. The advocates open themselves to affective intimacy with the one they are trying to help and with his family, becoming friends, counselors, and more. They not only participate in personal reciprocal exchanges, but also mediate between the family and the community at large—especially interceding with the police, the school, and the juvenile court.

The establishment of primary relations between the advocate and his young friend is aided by the fact that they share the same life conditions and cultural heritage, by the voluntary nature of the commitment on both sides, and by the lack of extrinsic motives or competing objectives on the part of the advocate. Advocates are not employees of an agency nor professionals whose lives are based outside the relationship in question or the community itself. The caring and commitment are readily seen as nonmanipulative, thus enhancing for the youth the attraction and influence of the advocate's values.

These values are family oriented. Center participants remind each other that as "children of God" they become brothers and sisters to one another, specifically committed to one another's well-being and to the full reciprocity that ideally characterizes natural families. The life of the center is not meant to displace participants' natural family ties, but to augment them, linking the homes, the center activities, the community at large, and the formal institutions and agencies of the society.

Sister Isolina believes that the marked ability of center adults to inspire young Playeros to strive for self-development lies in the presentation and acceptance of primary ties among all concerned. These relations derive from the community members' sensitivity to Christian imagery stressing the "Fatherhood of God"; in this concept of the human family, self-respect and respect for others are binding on all brothers and sisters. Families may disagree among themselves, but ultimately the members are committed to one another's welfare and are bound together by unique ties. In the context of this common Christian idealism, the activities of advocates in guiding others or acting on their behalf seem to grow naturally out of the stable, authentic commitments of people to their extended families. Accepting the center's philosophy that one has the capacity to change self or community is parallel to accepting the standards of any intimate primary group.

The essential features of the Umoja model are also found in the remarkable development in La Playa. There is a central figure who activates others; there is voluntary entry and exit, which reduces the sense of coercion for participants; the helped become in turn helpers, with the dignity of teaching and giving themselves. There is also a collective renaming process that crystallizes a new identity of self and others. New identities in turn are associated with a new belief in the capacity of the renamed to achieve their potential and in the capacity of the community to function as a successful collective, altering or preserving the terms of neighborhood life. The rehabilitation of deviants is fostered in much the same way as the restructuring of neighborhoods. At the very foundation of the model is the participants' view of their relations with one another as being primary, with the implicit promise of interpersonal support and common idealistic goals.

Any group with sufficient power over nonmembers can force them to approximate certain behavior, but compliance usually depends on how long effective control lasts. Rehabilitation of delinquency and revitalization of neighborhood structures, however, call for deeper, more enduring changes in the sense of self and the strivings of the conscious will. Such deep modification is most likely when people perceive one another as members of the same primary group, to which they are mutually committed and in which praise and blame signify the most. The use of family and kinship terms of address and the introduction of names (such as Umoja or Adella) that suggest a common heritage and group pride reinforce the sense of belonging and the chance of genuine, sustained conversion.

YOUTH-IN-ACTION

Principles of self-referral, mutual help exchanged between peers, nonauthoritarian leadership, reidentification, and the imagery of family-type relations among socially or culturally homogeneous people can be found at work in other community programs using local resources for local problems. One example of such a program is Youth-In-Action in Chester, Pennsylvania, approximately 13 miles south of Philadelphia on the Delaware River.

Chester, with a population of 53,000, has the appearance of a long-neglected community—neglected by private enterprise, by government agencies, and by the citizens of Chester. Here again are all the ingrained problems associated with urban density: poverty, high unemployment, lack of opportunities and resources, lack of local control over institutional decisions that affect the area, and crime, delinquency, drugs, and despair. Chester has the second highest crime rate in the state, more than 50 percent of the crimes being burglary, larceny or other property offenses. In addition to the fear generated by such extreme law enforcement problems, the economic impact of crime in Chester has been devastating. The unemployment rate is 17 percent in general and estimated at more than 20 percent in any given year for black males. Public assistance expenditures amount to more than $1 million per month in Chester.

As might be expected, the juvenile population of Chester is deeply affected by these economic and social ills. Of a total of 9,311 juveniles in 1976, 11 percent were arrested at least once and 210 remanded to the juvenile justice system. Regularly 15 percent of Chester's children never complete high school. Chester, they say, is "no place to be somebody."

In spite of the deep social problems and in marked contrast to official inertia, a dynamic program for youth and community development has been put together in Chester, entirely staffed by volunteer nonprofessionals. Founded in 1968 through the energy and vision of Tommie Lee Jones, the organization was known originally as the Black Youth Society and was entirely a self-funded operation run out of Mrs. Jones's home. Now incorporated as Youth-In-Action (YIA), the program runs on a continuing grant from Sun Oil plus some LEAA funds. The various activities and programs that have been organized or influenced by Youth-In-Action in Chester are now strongly endorsed by the social service agencies of Chester and of Delaware County, a testimony to the effectiveness of YIA efforts.

One of the first targets of YIA was the youth gangs multiplying in different areas of the city. The program worked with gang leaders and managed to bring together members of rival gangs to promote a spirit of coexistence and to eliminate the threat to community security from gang warfare. YIA began to coordinate alternative youth groups that could diminish the attraction of gangs. They also acted as mediators in gang disputes. Through the activities of YIA, the gang threat has been all but eliminated in the area.

Self-rehabilitation of former gang members, drug users, truants, and parolees takes place through peer counseling. The youths themselves, working with an ideal of self-development through service to the community and to one another, counsel each other on school, family, and legal problems. The obvious authenticity of the commitment to self-change made by those counseled develops from the genuine primary support made available through these peer relations. The counselors are youths who have been in the same kinds of trouble themselves and have been counseled in turn.

The youth counseling program has become so sophisticated that YIA has begun to take referrals from Delaware County Child Care Services and other youth agencies of the state, in addition to self-referrals. Activities include an outreach program for drug users and help for anyone who wants it with legal assistance agencies. YIA also actively counsels and assists truants.

The minority youths of Chester repeatedly encounter a variety of problems in their school careers. For example, many young people who were talented athletes were encouraged by high school coaches to take nonacademic courses that enabled them to devote more time to sports. At graduation, offers of college scholarships were withheld from these students or misplaced. Some students who sought to take advantage of a full athletic scholarship were unable to qualify on college placement exams.

Counseling about their education and mediation with school

authorities are now provided through YIA, which especially encourages students to continue their education or vocational training. YIA helps arrange financial assistance for students whenever possible. There is also a tutorial service to improve chances for college acceptance. The organization helps raise scholarships for higher education as well as funds for books, clothing, and other necessities. By 1973 YIA had fifty-eight college and vocational graduates to its credit—community children whom the organization had motivated and supported through various stages of their school careers.

Another target for Youth-In-Action was what they considered the "brain drain." The only options available for most of Chester's youth have been either to remain in the city and face stagnation in an environment vacant of opportunity, or to leave Chester in hope of finding advancement elsewhere. YIA sought to provide a third option: remain in Chester, but develop personally through assisting in the uplift of the community.

Families in Chester's low-income neighborhoods were among those also assisted by YIA. Many such families were without adequate food or shelter, even though 60 percent of the city's population received some form of public assistance. YIA found many cases where parents were acting out their frustrations by abusing or neglecting children. A range of community social problems frequently caused interruptions in income, leading to evictions and intrafamily quarrels that would often end in family court. YIA responded to this complex of problems with immediate material and psychological assistance for families in crisis. The help includes counseling, mediation in family arguments, and referrals to other family service agencies. During the flood of 1971, YIA was ready with assistance of all kinds—rescues, shelter, and the distribution of food and clothing. These same services are continuously available through YIA in the event of fire, eviction, illness, or other misfortune.

Other services to Chester carried out through YIA include field trips to acquaint youths with places and events of cultural significance—the Franklin Mint, the Black History Museum, the International Black Olympics, and many places of historical interest in the Philadelphia area. There is also a summer day care program, offering tutoring, swimming, and games. YIA has organized social events, dances, and sports, sending fifty Chester youths to the International Sports Program at Cheyney State College. A senior citizens program under YIA provides visiting, reading, shopping, and advocacy for older people. Recently YIA engaged young people in a clean-up of thirty city blocks of Chester, its parks, and its public facilities.

The social structure and the objectives and philosophy of Youth-In-Action closely approximate the Umoja model. Self-development, peer counseling, and community development are the major inter-related objectives pursued through the effective unity of an informal "brotherhood." Membership is mostly black (Chester is 65 percent black) and is made up entirely of people responding to the same conditions of deprivation. The relations between participants are personal, not professional or bureaucratic. These are people who recognize themselves in one another and offer mutual help.

The idealization of the group life holds out to members the promise of support and concern, but calls for the individual to strive to grow and to achieve. Service to others is seen as the expression of a well-developed person and provides the rehabilitative program of YIA. This service is obviously a concrete advantage to the community and constitutes an important source of pride to the group. More than an activist organization, YIA is a community family of youths who reinforce in one another a new, positive personal identity, who draw strength from one another, and who thus are able to sustain a broad range of activities on a shoestring. They are a community catalyst, stimulating many diverse groups in the area to work together on common problems. Here again is evidence of a multifaceted development in which neighborhood problems are attacked and social structures are glued back together in a process that also reconstructs and reinforces the skills and identities of the young people involved. The basis of authentic commitment appears to be the primary nature of the human ties maintained.

One young school dropout, with a history of arrest, violence, and abrasive hostility, was asked how he happened to be in YIA. His answer is significant: "I'm not the 'street kid' any more. I'm something else. They call me by a new name here; so I'm doing new things."

THE SOUTH ARSENAL NEIGHBORHOOD
DEVELOPMENT CORPORATION

The South Arsenal Neighborhood Development Corporation (SAND) was initiated in 1967 as the first neighborhood development corporation in Connecticut. It was conceived and managed entirely by residents of an inner city area located just north of Hartford's central business district.

In the mid 1960s the South Arsenal community was designated for urban renewal. Initially these were to be 640 new housing units, but during the Nixon administration the plans were cut back to 240 units, and many of the original South Arsenal residents found themselves displaced from their homes yet rejected as occupants of the new development. Many were bitter. For others, equally aroused, it was apparent that the wait for promised housing was to be much longer than anticipated.

As a result, local people began to hold meetings in homes and churches to discuss the situation and to organize committees to petition the bureaucracies of state and local governments. These neighborhood groups, eventually incorporated as SAND, were so united and clear about their objectives that the city was forced to deal with them, making at first small concessions and later giving more and more. SAND's pressure on the city has been responsible for the improvement of many city services in the South Arsenal area, including better street lighting. Today SAND is a recognized and respected negotiator among both residential and government committees.

Hartford has been the scene of costly gang violence linked, as in other cities, with the progressive deterioration of neighborhood structures and with the extensive breakdown of communications between resident groups—especially between the Hispanic and black communities. Hundreds of Hartford youths were directly involved in gang fighting. Strengthened by its success in mediating between community adults and the city, SAND began to mediate between different youth gangs, explaining to them they were merely giving the police cause to destroy them. This argument carried weight with the gangs since community members, young and old, felt the police had been totally insensitive to community needs.

Finally, frustration, fear, and confusion caused several members of a Hartford gang to come to SAND on their own asking for help. These boys had seen their friends and schoolmates shot in the street and had watched their own neighbors and families succumb to the terror of increasing gang warfare and the equally frightening counterwarfare of law enforcement officials. They felt a desire to do something positive for their community, but because of their own poor image as gang members, their efforts had been either ridiculed or ignored.

In response to this initiative, Carl Hardrick of SAND offered to work with the youths. His results have been outstanding. For the first time in local memory, dances and other social activities have been attended by rival gangs without guns, knives, or sticks. Eventually SAND, working in close cooperation with youth organizations, was able to begin putting the different ethnic communities in touch with each other, further reducing neighborhood tensions and building a broader base for community cooperation.

Hardrick argues that his success with Hartford "incorrigibles" has been based on his absolute honesty in dealing with them. Honesty fosters a spirit of mutual respect that has eased neighborhood tensions all around. When the fighting on the streets began to subside, the fighting in schools declined also. This work by SAND also draws on the principle of youths and neighbors helping each other to develop new ways of living. The young people of Hartford, previously condemned to self-destructive, often fatal involvement in violent gang action, now have a chance to develop as normal adolescents. Meanwhile, SAND continues to press for full economic revitalization of the South Arsenal neighborhood, from time to time joining its efforts to those of adjacent neighborhoods to increase the area and the total population served by its activities.

SAND's success can be measured by the substantial physical development since 1967. SAND has demonstrated an increasingly sophisticated ability to integrate and coordinate federal, state, and local government funds with private philanthropy and investment. SAND now owns and manages through a limited partnership (South Arsenal Neighborhood Associates) a 274-unit new housing development for low- and moderate-income families and the elderly. SAND was the prime mover in the construction of the internationally acclaimed SAND Everywhere School and in the renovation of Bellevue Square, a low-income public housing project. SAND has joined efforts with the city of Hartford to secure a neighborhood facility grant from the U.S. Department of Housing and Urban Development for the renovation of the former SAND warehouse as a multipurpose "Neighborhood Life Center."

SAND regards itself as concerned for the needs of all residents of its area, past, present, and future. One of its most popular programs, SHOP (SAND Home Orientation Program), has become a full-scale orientation project, counseling residents and newcomers to the area on all matters pertaining to housing, living, and working in South Arsenal. As a result of SHOP, the sense of a genuine community with mutual support is strong in South Arsenal. SAND, building on the structure of community relations it has developed, is continuing to sponsor participatory community planning and to merge community interests with outside public and private interests.

The vitality of SAND is its most remarkable characteristic—its capacity to keep renewing itself and to take on projects of increasing scope and complexity. SAND's success must be viewed in relation to the sustained, willing commitment of its members. This solidarity now transcends subcultural differences between blacks and Hispanics and is based in part on a common perception of shared problems and interests. But the strength and persistence of the cooperative effort suggests its roots in deeper sociopsychological structures—in the nonprofessional, voluntary, self-actualizing aspects of the program and the strict use of local talent.

The social base of SAND is the neighborhood itself; the staff is not drawn from a professional agency or organization, and volunteers do not serve a bureaucracy based outside the community and oriented to its own interests. SAND people are local people who endure local problems together, who develop primary kinds of identification, support, and communication, and who cooperate closely in sustained effort. Local people, under their own direction, are solving local problems that were thought to be manageable only by professionals, who deemed local control inappropriate.

The concrete benefits of safer streets and better schools and housing are apparent, but equally important to SAND neighbors are the benefits of increased self-respect and mutual respect that grow from their successful joint efforts. The participants feel that they are "in this together," that they are in charge of the terms of their own existence, and that together they are capable of finding ways to do what ought to be done. These feelings sustain the ideals and interchanges that are transforming the South Arsenal ghetto. SAND differs in emphasis from the activities in Chester, La Playa, and Umoja, but shares the basic features cited.

CONCLUSION

Juvenile justice in America operates within a special kind of paradox. It is a system of keepers and captives, but it is currently committed to an ideology of concern for the delinquent himself—the desire to "save" the captive child. Although we may "do well" sometimes, "doing good" presents special difficulties. To do good to another, especially against his will, is the paradox of corrections.

Regardless of the intrinsic value of the objectives of the would-be benefactor, the "beneficiary," especially if he is a captive, finds his own special coherence of self and world invaded. Juvenile rehabilitation programs are organized for the direct purpose of replacing the captive's own self-understanding with values, adjustments, even loyalties that are selected by the captor for the other's "good." Those identifications that are the special consequence of the captive's salient status and life encounters are denigrated in the service of the sanctioned rationality of the dominant part in this association of unequals. The giving and receiving are unidirectional. The two confront each other as strangers, often bearing mutually exclusive social identities; differences of race, education, socioeconomic status, age, and culture raise barriers to communication and commitment. Keepers and captives are outsiders to each other's worlds. A captor who intends deliberately to excise important chunks of his alien captive's identity can expect resistance.

To invent a juvenile justice system and to commit it to any version of treatment, correction, or rehabilitation is to perpetuate this paradox of coercive resocialization masterminded by captors and imposed on captives. However well policy is supported by the grounded reasoning of social science, it remains rhetoric more persuasive to correction agents than to clientele. However closely "good reasons" of behavioral science may be interpreted into specifics of action (and there is a considerable gap between theory and deed), the principals of the juvenile justice drama—delinquents and social workers—confront each other as unequals in power, in prestige, in initiative, and in dignity derived from identity labels.

Accordingly, community-based groups, are more readily accepted as primary by the juvenile than are juvenile justice programs. Such community groups take on functions historically assigned to families. They mediate between the community and its youths and, in so doing, truly modify the young people, many of whom have been the "scandal" of juvenile justice programs. They draw the community youths into positive, reconstructive activities that serve the needs of the community while enabling the youths to recognize and accept new, positive ways of being themselves in their own neighborhoods, among their own people.

Old identities are revalued, cleansed of some traits while others become symbols of self-respect and the basis of new ways of participating in familiar scenes. With the close participation of the individual, old identities are refashioned in a process supported by family intimacy. Established and clarified are social norms that will relate the youth functionally to society at large and specifically to his own ghetto. Neither the youths nor the ghetto are seen as having negative characteristics that are fixed, but both are envisioned as moving toward the realization of their inherent positive characteristics. This vision, shaped by peer approval and the intrinsic rewards of primary group life, is translated into direct action that can readily quicken a congruent community response.

These programs are not a complete substitute for other social agency activity, nor do they signal the end of government responsibility for dealing with the social programs and needs of inner city areas, but they do make a particular contribution that warrants the respect and support of other agencies. These programs are achieving a significant success—as defined by the objectives of juvenile justice—with the young minority group least well served by existing official approaches. Indigenous programs make an equally gratifying contribution in meeting the community needs of urban centers and their occupants. Certainly continuing research into these and hundreds of similar community programs is in order, and I believe it will confirm and strengthen the analysis made here.

REFERENCES

1. Roger Martinson, "What Works?—Questions and Answers about Prison Reform," *Public Interest*, 35 (Spring 1974):22.
2. From "Field Interviews," unpublished transcript of a tape recording, New York, June 14, 1977, Washington, D.C., American Enterprise Institute, Mediating Structures Project.
3. Ibid.

6 MEDIATING STRUCTURES AND PUBLIC POLICY

In the preceding chapters, I have attempted to describe, analyze, and interpret the resourcefulness of local mediating institutions successfully addressing a myriad of social problems—especially youth crime—that have defied solution by some of the more traditional, professionally oriented approaches. Crime and the fear of crime are major obstacles to business and residential redevelopment in the central city and erode the economic base of the community. I have delineated the characteristics of local programs that enable them to combat this problem by profoundly influencing the lives of youngsters.

These mediating institutions give youngsters a sense of identity, a sense of direction, and a purpose in life. The framework within which individual expectations are established and enforced also serves the neighborhood at large. The difficult task that remains is to employ the energy of this new-found human capital to rebuild the economic wasteland in which many of these programs exist.

No matter how creative and imaginative the efforts of these mediating structures, their impact will be lost unless public policy allows them to fulfill their potential. People at the local level are beginning to take control of their own lives and insist on managing their own affairs in accordance with their own perceived self-interest. Neighborhood people are developing a new perspective on their own role and

109

responsibilities. As they redefine themselves, they seek parity with the policy "experts" and political opinion makers, who represent conflicting interests.

In the contention between politician and expert, the politicians have the power, whereas the opinion of experts may merely be prophecy. If the people's will is wrong, the politician is very much aware that the people are likely to blame the politicians who gave them the poisoned apple rather than blame themselves for having asked for it. But expert prophecy cannot match the political sense that something is on the minds of the people. Whether the mind set of the people is contradictory or not, public policy must cater to the politician's sense of the popular will.

We cannot discuss the possibility of using mediating structures to minimize crime and urban decay without understanding that policy makers see these structures as a *consequence* of urban distress. The following sections trace the history of this relationship.

PRE-1930s POLICY

The family and the tribe or village have been the subjects of public policy in most societies throughout most of mankind's existence— even when the goal of public policy has been the gratification of a ruling class. Only in industrial societies of the past 200 years has public policy addressed the individual, and only in recent times in the United States has the individual become the predominant concern of public policy. Modern industrial societies—whether East or West, North or South, socialist or democratic—base their social policies on the legacy of eighteenth-century European liberalism, which freed industrial labor from the ties of clan and village. Under the liberal notion that men (and women and children) were free to contract their labor, industrial laborers broke the paternalistic bonds of the older social order. No longer did a feudal lord offer protection in return for fiefdom, and no longer were the family and village of a person's birth the only determinants of the individual's position in society.

In the United States the social policy of the 1930s was clearly the work of professional politicians who were mindful of both the individualist's creed and the currents of reform. Reformers have always been active in America, but proposals for government intervention in the economic system met with little success until the crisis of the 1930s. At that time the breakdown of the ability of families to provide for their needy, particularly their elderly, opened the way for the New Deal. In 1930 there were 6.5 million persons over the age of sixty-five, and most of them were supported by relatives. No more than 100,000 persons had any sort of pension, and no more than 100,000 were cared for in poorhouses.

With 12 million workers left jobless in the crisis, the system of caring for the elderly was severely strained. Even though the elderly did not raise massive political protests, the New Dealers quickly responded to their problem because it was a fundamental breach of the code that envisioned a nation of strong individuals. Paralleling this breach was an awareness of abundance. Despite unemployment rates that averaged 29 percent during the decade, many persons were obviously unaffected. That the code could break down for some and leave the system intact for others raised a serious issue, and government intervention seemed the only solution. The development of a professional class of social policy bureaucrats was the inevitable by-product of the crisis. How this product has survived into more recent times is best illustrated in the development of the Great Society.

Government programs expanded enormously after World War II. Public confidence in the federal government grew as a result of its success with the New Deal programs and the war effort. Without serious objection, the government was relied on to smooth the integration of veterans into postwar society and to convert the war economy to peaceful prosperity. More and more the government was called into service for particular purposes and for special interest groups. It became the champion of all, not merely the needy.

In more recent times government has directed hundreds of billions of dollars to programs to upgrade American cities. Massive funds have also been spent on highways, suburban housing, income transfer, and social services. Local governments in particular became dependent on federal programs. In 1950 local governments received $2 billion in federal aid, which increased to $7 billion in 1960 and $11 billion in 1965. Yet it is doubtful whether present urban conditions are any better for the effort. American cities are still faced with enormous problems: middle-class flight to the suburbs, erosion of economic and tax bases, deterioration of housing, decline of the quality of life, and more. In addition to these decades-old concerns,

some cities—particularly in the Northeast and industrial Midwest—
now confront a worsening economic trend.

Why after so much effort and money, are the problems of the
cities still with us? One answer is that currently there is no national
policy that can accommodate the diversity of neighborhood needs
and create a strong and comprehensive set of programs to save the
victims of urban blight. An alternative to the pattern of patching
up and quieting down urban neighborhoods is needed. No policy
framework exists to provide guidance to local officials on the best
programmatic means to solve their problems; no one knows what
works and what does not. There is a need to develop a policy concept that is sufficiently comprehensive to deal with the varied systemic problems of different cities and neighborhoods.

Before such a policy can be formulated, however, it is necessary to
review and evaluate the multiplicity of programs and policies that
already exist or have been attempted. A rigorous and comprehensive
study of the urban and neighborhood systems must be undertaken
to determine what has been learned from past efforts before a new
solution to the problems can be created.

Since 1968 a policy framework has begun to emerge as neighborhoods throughout the country have rallied to work for their own
renewal. This movement has evolved in older industrial centers, but
unlike the poverty programs of the 1960s, it has not depended on
federal initiative alone. The impetus has come from local groups
organized spontaneously, block by block, to save their own neighborhoods. Black clubs, community organizations, and neighborhood
associations have begun to deal with housing decay, mortgage redlin-
ing, deterioration of city services, ever higher property tax rates,
crime and vandalism, and the disruption of neighborhoods by block-
busting, urban renewal, and expressways.

Since 1975 the same groups that first organized around local issues
have coalesced into a major national neighborhood lobby. The political power of this new lobby has been recognized by many in Congress. For example, under intense pressure from neighborhood
organizations, Congress in 1975 passed the Home Mortgage Disclo-
sure Act, and in 1976 2,000 neighborhood organizers and citizen
leaders met in Washington to endorse the National Neighborhood
Policy Act. The potential for political support was recognized by
the Ford administration, which organized White House conferences
on neighborhood revitalization.

Ironically, public officials, policy makers, and the press around the country often confuse this new movement with Great Society programs. It is not uncommon for public officials to refuse to support citizen involvement in urban problems because it seems to resemble the programs of the 1960s, or they find a proposed neighborhood-based urban strategy unacceptable for fear the community organizations would in turn engage in advocacy programs or the delivery of services.

Those who confuse the War on Poverty with the neighborhood movement are mistaken. To clarify the issue I shall briefly examine the origins of the Great Society programs and the criticisms of them. The intent of this analysis is to put in clearer perspective the neighborhood movement of the 1970s and to present urban poverty as a subject for public discussion and legislative action.

POVERTY PROGRAMS OF THE 1960s

During the 1960s, the plight of the American cities—particularly the inner cities—was labeled a "crisis," and there were frequent references to anarchy, radical change, crime in the streets, and the breakdown of law and order. Although it is true that violence occurs with increasing frequency in many American slums, the conditions that give rise to inner city violence have existed for a long time. The rhetoric of crisis in the 1960s did not center on such critical urban problems as air and water pollution, intrametropolitan job dispersal, housing obsolescence, real estate management practices, the mismatch between municipal and state fiscal systems, demographic changes, transportation, taxation, and education. The word "crisis" reflected then, as it does today, a fear of black violence.

By 1966 the mood of crisis elicited a somewhat frenzied series of responses in the nation's cities, including massive police and military actions, repressive laws, and quickly conceived crash programs for employment, housing, and public welfare. Most of these programs were aimed at cooling off the so-called crisis; many have been ineffective, if not irrelevant. Some, instead of alleviating the problems, have actually created further frustrations.

New legislation directed at problems of race, delinquency, urban and rural poverty, unemployment, and the physical deterioration of inner cities included the Area Redevelopment Act, amendments to the Social Security Act, the Manpower Development Act, the Elementary and Secondary Education Act, the Voter Registration Act, the Juvenile Delinquency Act, amendments to the Housing Act, the Civil Rights Act, the Economic Opportunity Act (EOA), and Model Cities programs incorporated in the Demonstration Cities Act. Thus, the 1960s saw the federal government explicitly commit itself to a struggle against poverty and racial discrimination.[1] Johnson's War on Poverty was principal among the social innovations of this era. Sar Levitan, John Donovan, and others point to the 1964 Economic Opportunity Act as symbolizing, more than any other piece of social legislation during this period, the Great Society's commitment to the nation's poor.[2] The announced aim was not only to eliminate poverty but to restructure societal institutions by giving the poor a chance to design and administer programs. Much of this new legislation could be considered a unique form of class legislation. As Sar Levitan notes:

> The Economic Opportunity Act is unabashedly class legislation, designating a special group in the population as eligible to receive the benefits of the law. There is, of course, nothing new in class legislation; our laws are replete with provisions that benefit one group or another. Normally these groups banded into organizations to assure that the rights or special privileges granted them by the laws were preserved. The novelty of the E.O.A. lay in the fact that the poor were not represented by trade or other conventional organizations. Welfare agencies, public or private, could hardly claim to represent the poor though they could and did insist that they did a great deal for the poor, if not with them.[3]

The experiences of the 1960s stimulated new criticism by social scientists, policy analysts, and the general public of federal social policy and social service programs. Michael Svirdoff, in the 1969 Ford Foundation Annual Report, noted that the policies and programs of the 1960s aimed exclusively at poverty and racism were appropriate and necessary in the short run but may have had unfortunate consequences in the long run:

> The polarization that today puts American Society under strain stems in large part from the dissatisfactions of whites in the near poor, lower middle class and middle classes, those left out of much recent public programming. This predominatly working class sector has since the thirties been a prime beneficiary of government programs and legislation—Social Security, the National Labor Relations Act, federal housing, and even highway programs. Never-

theless, they see themselves as paying a disproportionate amount of both the social and monetary costs of the innovations of the sixties.[4]

Donovan states that although the Economic Opportunity Act did not constitute the entire War on Poverty, it was presented to the public as such. Thus, its symbolic significance is great, and it has influenced attitudes toward the poor and toward social policies of the past decade.[5] For example, Charles Grosser states, "Ironically, the anti-poverty programs, having failed to solve the problems of the minority poor, are now perceived by the white working class to be the source of the inequities from which it suffers." Grosser concludes that "the programs themselves and the people whose grievances they failed to redress have become scapegoats for the anguish, distress, and disillusionment of the white working class."[6]

Concerned public officials, journalists, and scholars feel that the Economic Opportunity Act created a welfare backlash, primarily among blue-collar and service workers. These policy analysts point out that the War on Poverty created an illusion among working Americans that the poor would be placed in decent jobs and houses while white "middle Americans" would have to scrape along. This phenomenon, according to Harold Wilensky and Charles Lebeaux, Amitai Etzioni, Lee Rainwater, and others, produced a "narrow" backlash—a negative reaction toward social policies aimed at a particular group of disadvantaged people.[7] This backlash was directed primarily toward programs designed to aid black people. Etzioni claims that these attitudes do not influence other welfare reforms. He points out that domestic programs catering to only one group— farmers, users of highways, blacks, or the poor—tend to be much less popular than those that are believed to benefit everyone, such as federal aid to education or Social Security.[8]

A working alliance between social and political scientists, policy analysts, politicians, foundation executives, federal bureaucrats, and others attempted to forge a national effort to master the complexities of social, economic, and regional problems. But within five years these alliances broke down, and public support for the War on Poverty dramatically abated. Programs oriented toward serving the poor were perceived as primarily for poor blacks. Subjective evaluations of the programs were harsh. In 1968 Tom Wicker commented that the War on Poverty, "somehow managed to wind up alienating many of the black poor, as well as white conservatives . . . and members of

Congress."[9] Lee Rainwater notes that the Economic Opportunity Act made promises to the black community and, through a pseudo-radical rhetoric, angered and insulted the working class, while it delivered no more than symbolic resources to black people. Rainwater argues that the initial sympathy that many working-class people extended to the poor and (more grudgingly) to blacks was reversed as the 1960s wore on. He states, "Originally, the working class assumed that these groups were simply trying to shift the odds so that they would have a better chance to achieve a mainstream existence. They further assumed that this existence would be achieved by the same combination of personal hard work and good luck that they feel for themselves."[10]

Miller and Altschuler contend that efforts to improve the circumstances of the poor will inevitably affect the groups that are economically and socially contiguous to the poor. They explain that in 1968 the people with incomes between $3,450 (for a family of four—the 1968 poverty line) and approximately $10,000 (the U.S. Bureau of Labor Statistics set $9,750 as an "adequate but modest standard") felt ignored and neglected. They claim that those feelings arose from the War on Poverty, which gave workers in this income range the sense that they were "picking up the tab" for the poor.

> Indeed, many feel that they are "put upon" by these efforts at change, bearing the burdens with little support and aid from society at large. The likelihood is that these non-affluent but non-poor groups will be calling for social services and other aids for themselves. Not only will they be seeking social services as mobility aids (for they too feel that their and their children's economic mobility is limited) but they will call for social services as basic amenities to which they have a claim. If, for example, Headstart classes and day care become increasingly widespread in poverty neighborhoods, why should the neighborhoods of the not-so-well-to-do lack such amenities and benefits.[11]

Herbert Gans points out that white working-class people feel that vociferous black militants have blackmailed federal and local governments into dividing the economic pie so that the share of blue-collar neighborhoods goes to the ghetto. He adds that in the 1950s government did little directly in behalf of either the white working class or the ghetto poor; in the 1960s, particularly after the ghetto rebellions, they instituted programs for the ghetto while still doing almost nothing—or at least nothing new—for working-class constituents.

According to Gans, whites have considerably exaggerated this new distribution of governmental resources, for the ghetto has not benefited significantly from governmental antipoverty programs. Thus, he concludes, working-class people may feel relative deprivation; they are not getting as much in new resources from the public economy as the blacks, and they are not getting as much from the private economy as the middle class.[12]

Other analysts feel that the policies of the 1960s contradicted the American work ethic and other beliefs, thus augmenting working-class malaise. *Newsweek*'s in-depth report on white Americans points out that blacks are perceived by many whites as morally different, as circumventing the rules of the Protestant ethic. Furthermore, government policies such as the War on Poverty are seen to support this nonwork ethic and to create conditions in which blacks do not have to work very hard, if at all, for what they get. *Newsweek*, through a commissioned Gallup Poll, found that whites felt blacks were receiving too much too soon and that blacks had a better chance to succeed than whites. Further, the study reports that the majority of whites see public welfare and War on Poverty programs as oriented exclusively toward black people.[13]

Such conjectures do not adequately explain the alleged discontent, nor is it clear whether working-class resentment is any different in quality or quantity from that of any other group. Indeed, a careful analysis of the War on Poverty reveals that the bulk of the poor remained untouched by its programs. One of the major difficulties was that self-help, bootstrap programs, while desirable in themselves, had been superimposed on a welfare system that had been designed to deal with the economic and social problems of the 1930s and was totally inadequate for contemporary needs.

In its discussion of government programs, the *Report of the National Advisory Commission on Civil Disorders*[14] indicated that the present welfare system contributes materially to the tensions and the social disorganization that have contributed to urban riots and the breakup of neighborhoods. Of the many reasons for this seeming paradox, two stand out: (1) government programs do not reduce the powerlessness of their recipients, since they are usually controlled by the nonpoor; and (2) the programs have often raised aspiration levels without materially raising standards of living. The second factor gives rise to the sense of relative deprivation and may explain why many government programs created to remedy urban problems have actually helped perpetuate them by increasing frustration and hopelessness among urban residents.

Although these factors are significant, the principal reason for the failures of urban policies and programs is that the systemic origins of urban decline have not been clearly recognized; the prerequisites for effective change have not been met. It has not been recognized that the deterioration of cities is rooted in institutionalized policies, attitudes, and practices; instead, the tendency has often been to respond to symptoms. Structured into the system in most cities are processes that discriminate against individuals on the basis of race or that discriminate against entire communities on the basis of their physical properties. When either inequity is operating, tensions between the races will increase, and the decline of the city will accelerate.

A second reason for the persistent failure of urban programs has been the tendency to tackle the problem on a large scale. Virtually all efforts to halt the decline of cities fail to define national policy initiatives that serve the varied needs of differing neighborhoods. To meet realistically the preconditions for effective change, it must be recognized that the neighborhood—not the sprawling, anonymous metropolis—is the key. People live in neighborhoods, not cities; their investments, emotional as well as economic, are in neighborhoods, not cities. And the city cannot survive if its neighborhoods continue to decline.

THE NEIGHBORHOOD AS A
FOCUS FOR POLICY

The past decades have witnessed enormous growth—suburban expansion within regions, movement toward the sun belt, growth in social programs, and of course growth in population and gross national product. Government policies have stimulated this growth at the expense of existing communities. For example, many suburbs derive all the benefits of urban life while remaining exempt from all the costs of restrictive zoning, inequitable revenue arrangements, and artificial municipal boundaries. The viability of the neighborhood has been undermined by policies promoting suburban and sun belt expansion, with little effort to shore up established neighborhoods, and by the bureaucratization of daily life on an ever more alienating scale within cities. Economically and culturally, too, we have created a throwaway society. While suburban sprawl devours productive land, the small-scale living unit within the large metropolis—the neighbor-hood—has been abandoned. Most significantly, the welter of govern-ment programs has been put forth in a policy vacuum. The response to the urban plight has been scattershot programs directed at symp-toms, without a serious policy framework. Consequently, existing programs often work at cross purposes. Government subsidizes sub-urban sprawl as well as housing rehabilitation; the real estate ads tout the benefits of subsidized mortgages on outer fringe housing develop-ments while policy makers wonder what happened to the demand for middle-income housing in the older neighborhoods. Government promotes the economic development of older cities, even as tax gimmicks permit newer areas to raid industry. The distributional effects of policies designed for macrostimulus are often ignored. The human problems of our neighborhoods, cities, suburbs, and farms are closely linked.

Neither policy nor rhetoric coherently addresses the interde-pendency of the interests of the region and the neighborhood. Few, if any, national leaders are discussing inducements to people to stay and reinvest in their communities. There is no national growth policy to guide state and local officials on how best to serve the mutual self-interests of interstate and substate regions, cities, and neighborhoods. Generally, reform efforts to improve governmental accountability get bogged down in the controversy over centralization as opposed to decentralization. Some believe governmental effectiveness can be brought about only through the aggregation of political and ad-ministrative power at the level of metropolitan regions. Others take the opposite position that greater governmental responsive-ness can be achieved by disaggregating power to cities and their neighborhoods.

The difficulty is that no one has yet figured out how to deal successfully with the total system. Traditionally, Washington has dealt with symptoms without an understanding of the limitations of any proposed solution. It has not been recognized that the larger the solution, the bigger the potential unintended problems and con-sequences. For example, in the 1930s the Dust Bowl was saved, but millions of farmers were not. Today our agricultural surpluses keep half the world alive, but the American family farm is dying. The

Federal Housing Authority, the Highway Transportation Act, public housing, and many other policies defined nationally have resolved one part of the problem, but at the expense of local neighborhoods.

Growth policies, governmental structures, and social programs must all address the question of *scale*. In the urban setting, it is the neighborhood that permits a strong social fabric and the mediating institutions that de Toqueville hailed as enabling American democracy to thrive. It is easy and fashionable to blame urban blight entirely on demographics, but in many communities vital, well-organized neighborhoods have flourished in the face of poverty, little education, and physical deterioration. In response to cold data alone, well-intentioned attempts—such as bureaucratic income transfers, delivery of "services," or razing of blighted buildings—have often ignored the social structure of the communities. It is now well established that urban renewal usually made life worse for the average resident. Less obviously, the same can be said of many social programs and development subsidies. The bureaucratization of functions best performed locally saps the community's natural coping mechanisms, defeats voluntarism, and promotes alienation.

If there is one lesson to be learned from the neighborhood movement, it is the need for appropriate scale. The question is not one of absolute size but, rather, of what size is appropriate for the job. Small is not necessarily better than large, nor is neighborhood necessarily better than city or region. Some activities are best carried out on a broader basis than the neighborhood to allow economies of scale to come into play. But people for their different purposes need many different structures, both small and large, some exclusive and some comprehensive. Small-scale administration, though contrary to the cost-effective notions of contempory public administration, can in some cases achieve results comparable to those of the centralized approach and at a lower cost. In short, economy of scale means small scale as often as it means large scale.

NEIGHBORHOOD APPROACHES TO SERVICE DELIVERY

Professionals have earnestly sought to bring services into the community arena. During the past decade, however, in spite of significant reforms and many important research efforts, providers and consumers have not been satisfied. Many still claim that the delivery of services is fragmented, often inefficient, duplicative, and bureaucratically confusing and that the delivery systems lack accountability and do not meet the needs of the poor. In part, these shortcomings stem from a lack of knowledge concerning how different groups of people solve problems and cope with crises. Further, service delivery systems are often developed without regard to the unique elements of community and neighborhood life.

The efficacy of a service delivery system depends largely on understanding the context in which it operates. Although important work has been done to link services to poor neighborhoods, the results have been disappointing. Despite the rhetoric supporting community involvement, bureaucrats have shown little real understanding of the dynamics of urban life.

During the past two decades, human problems have been defined in the context of macrosocial and economic forces. It was believed that poverty was the central issue and that innovations were needed to reform social institutions and provide opportunities for mobility for poor people, particularly for blacks. By the late 1960s, however, there was widespread disillusionment with the effectiveness of Great Society programs, and the first Nixon administration began to dismantle these earlier initiatives because of their alleged inefficiency.

The service initiatives and theoretical systems of the 1960s and early 1970s were not directed toward the macroaspects of problem solving in a neighborhood context. Nor were these efforts explicitly directed to the universal problems of inequality, social injustice, and exclusion. In the 1960s these issues had been given attention only within the context of poverty; in the 1970s they were not even discussed.

A recurring theme has been the search for new models for the delivery of services; instead, new analysis is needed. First and foremost, a neighborhood approach requires the involvement of all concerned sectors in a city. Second, if it is to be successful, it must be pluralistic to meet the diverse needs of different groups of people. Money is not and should not be the prime consideration in altering the ways in which services are delivered. The discomfort of America's urban population is not entirely quantifiable by the cost of services or fee-for-service rates, and the profound sense of alienation that pervades cities—the feelings of powerlessness, meaninglessness, isolation, and self-estrangement—has no price tag. The question is whether the roots of alienation can be found in the neighborhood and whether changes in the delivery of services can help reverse or negate those alienating elements of community life.

Many neighborhood-based efforts fail in two ways: first, they do not deal directly with the issue of devolving power to citizens on a neighborhood level; and second, the administration of the formal system is not consistently responsive to the needs of different groups of people. Resource allocation must be a fundamental component of any strategy to devolve power. Policies that do not consider the ways in which citizens can control the allocation of resources are inadequate.

All public and private agencies in some way or other allocate resources to neighborhoods. Money and services are usually distributed to different districts on the basis of need as perceived by a small number of decision makers. The criteria for defining need are determined by complex administrative, political, and economic forces, often having little to do with the true needs of a particular neighborhood as seen by its inhabitants.

In contrast, citizens determine their own resource needs quite subjectively, using criteria that differ from those of the professional. In assessing needs, citizens are guided by two interrelated principles: equity and self-sufficiency.

Equity

The principle of equity is seen by citizens in two ways: whether their investment (objective or subjective) is equal to their return; and whether their neighborhood is getting its fair share of resources compared with other parts of the city. Thus, when citizens invest through the tax system, they expect a return in services and amenities. The difficulty, however, is that the return is not within the complete control of the citizens or even local decision makers.

On a local level, actual or perceived states of inequity have significant consequences. For example, if residents have sufficient resources, they will move out of the neighborhood and refuse to invest in it socially, physically, or economically. In other cases, residents may feel threatened by those of inferior social and economic status and as a result display increased hostility toward those, particularly in minority groups, considered too different. If a local agency projects an appearance of responsiveness but does not fully permit power to be shared, people feel cheated and manipulated. The result is an apartheid system of services in which minorities receive inadequate care while poor and working-class whites are caught between being too poor to afford their own physicians and being unwilling to attend a public-supported center.

Self-Sufficiency

Adherence to this principle allows people to participate in the system of social services and to exercise enough control over the services to deal successfully with the problems confronting their community. When these conditions do not exist, alienation may reach a level at which it has a negative effect on perceptions of self and of one's neighborhood.

The degree to which people feel self-sufficient is often determined by how the neighborhood defines itself and how others define it. Neighborhoods with strong ethnic, racial, or class identities often have great ability to deal with their problems. Such neighborhoods have a unique sense of pride, which affects the way they resolve difficulties. Yet public officials and scholars often refer to these communities in condescending, even pejorative terms, and policy makers neither build on the strengths of the neighborhood nor understand neighborhood social and cultural dynamics.

Of critical importance for the development of linkages between service delivery systems and neighborhoods is the social infrastructure of the neighborhood—that is, the neighborhood-based networks, such as social, civic, and cultural organizations, that can increase accountability between the system and the citizens. When such networks do not operate effectively little citizen involvement and much mistrust between consumers and providers of services can be expected.

Although important work has been done to link service delivery to neighborhoods, little consideration has been given to neighborhoods with multiethnic and multiracial populations. The intercultural dimension of neighborhood life, particularly as it relates to service delivery, is not fully understood. Too often delivery systems bypass neighborhood-based cultural and organizational networks with the potential to support services.

The problem is made more complex because it is not yet known empirically what the possibilities and ramifications of the interdependencies of race, ethnicity, social class, and well-being are for neighborhood service delivery.

Traditional solutions that rely on grants-in-aid should not be used; an economy that is based only on grants will not make it in the long run. Grants should be used for investment and leverage instead of for further expenditures. It is necessary to know who the real beneficiaries are and who in effect controls the grants and to focus on the structural problems that determine the flow of capital.

In addition, consideration should be given to the role of neighborhood-based organizations, institutions, or networks. Currently such entities are forced into one of two positions. As service delivery from larger public agencies breaks down, neighborhood-based institutions must organize themselves either to replace these institutions or to change them. For example, when credit is not available in a community or the number of jobs declines, neighborhood-based organizations may organize either for economic development or for the delivery of services. Similarly, when access to traditional institutions is denied or they no longer function effectively, neighborhood organizations may adopt strategies of advocacy or work toward changing those institutions.

REFERENCES

1.   The dramatic rise of social service programs has been documented by S.M. Miller and A. Altschuler in *Services for People: Report of the Task Force on Organization of Social Services,* U.S. Department of Health, Education and Welfare, February 1968.

2.   John Donovan, *The Politics of Poverty* (New York: Pegasus, 1967); Sar Levitan, *The Great Society's Poor Law: A New Approach to Poverty* (Baltimore: The Johns Hopkins Press, 1969).

3.   Levitan, *The Great Society's Poor Law,* pp. ix and 112.

4.   Michael Svirdoff, *The Ford Foundation Annual Report* (New York: Ford Foundation, 1969), p. 19.

5.   Donovan, *The Politics of Poverty,* p. 97.

6.   Charles Grosser, "Organizing in the White Community," *Social Work* 16, no. 3 (July 1971): 27.

7.   See for example, Amitai Etzioni, "A Moving to the Right," *Transaction* 77, no. 11 (September 1970): 4; and Harold Wilensky and Charles Le-

beaux, *Industrial Society and Social Welfare* (New York: Free Press, 1965).

8. Etzioni, "A Moving to the Right," p. 18.
9. Daniel Moynihan, *Perspectives on Poverty: On Understanding Poverty* (New York: Basic Books, 1968), p. 35. See also the *New York Times,* (July 28, 1968): editorial page.
10. Lee Rainwater, "Making the Good Life: Working Class Family and Life Style," unpublished manuscript, October 1970, p. 25.
11. Miller and Altschuler, *Services for People,* p. 9.
12. Herbert Gans, "Anxiety and Anger in the White Working Class: Some Hypotheses and Research Suggestions," unpublished manuscript, 1970, p. 3.
13. "The Troubled American," *Newsweek* (October 6, 1969): 29–68. See also Walter Walker, "The War on Poverty and the Poor: A Study of Race, Poverty and a Program" PH.D. dissertation, Brandeis University, 1970.
14. *Report of the National Advisory Commission on Civil Disorders,* Washington, D.C., March 1, 1968.

7 POLICY RECOMMENDATIONS

In this review of past and current approaches to the control and prevention of youth crime, I have discussed policies and programs that have evolved over decades of searching for solutions to crime and urban decline. Federal dollars primed the pumps of the vast array of university-based research efforts, traditional public and private social work, and mental health agencies that make up the complex of juvenile delinquency prevention and child welfare. More than thirty-four federal programs spend $2.5 billion a year to address the needs of children who are likely to be removed from their homes. In addition, billions of dollars are spent by state and local programs to care for such children, and the cost continues to escalate.

This expenditure has not improved the condition of our society, but has instead exacerbated the very problems these programs were designed to solve. Continued support of these traditional delivery systems, which view those in need of help as "clients," will lead to continued failure and worsening of the conditions that breed despair. The solution is not merely to improve coordination among bureaucratic agencies, nor is it to decentralize and restructure bureaucracies, redistributing to the states and localities the power and responsibilities accumulated in Washington. There must be a renegotiation of the values and interest on which public policies are established. The context in which policy is developed must be rearranged so that the interest, point of view, and condition of those "served" determine the nature of the help given and the manner in which it is disbursed.

Donald and Rachel Warren of Oakland University in Rochester, Michigan, in studies on neighborhoods, determined that 80 percent of the low-income residents in Detroit, when faced with a crisis, turned to individuals or institutions within their neighborhood for help.[1] These findings were confirmed by a study conducted by the University of Southern California (Washington campus), which asked people who had been in distress to list whom they turned to first.[2] The seven most frequently listed people were within the neighborhood (such as ministers, friends, hairdressers), and the eighth category was professional assistance, which was turned to after all other local resources had been exhausted.

It has been clearly demonstrated that informal networks (mediating structures) have the strength to solve a range of social problems that have defied solution by traditional bureaucratic organizations. Yet public policy continues to ignore these indigenous institutions and instead vests most of its resources in the institutions that neighborhood residents rank as their last choice. Traditional policy makers are heavily influenced by a set of negative assumptions about neighborhoods and are conditioned to study pathology. The National Institute of Mental Health reports that for every single study of the strengths of the American family, *ten* research projects are funded to study the pathology of the family. Such research serves to confirm these negative assumptions. Thus, the rescue strategies designed by service providers from outside the "diseased" environment have predictably negative results. As Mark Twain said, "When the only tool you have is a hammer, every problem looks like a nail."

The policy recommendations presented here are intended to protect the natural functions of mediating structures. They are consistent with the minimalist proposition set forth in the monograph *To Empower People*, that public policy should not interfere with mediating structures.[3] Perhaps this proposition should be elevated to the first law of public policy, borrowing from the Hippocratic Oath," I promise to do no harm."

The second proposition of the mediating structure paradigm is that mediating structures should be used to fulfill some public purpose. This presents both a challenge and an opportunity. The socioeconomic gap between the traditional service providers and those customarily labeled clients makes it difficult for the essential partnership to develop. Professionals often fail to understand or refuse to accept phenomena that are outside their own experience or that do not fit their own theories; the terms of the partnership require skills they do not possess. The so-called clients often surrender their autonomy and their own judgment in the mistaken belief that professionally trained experts know what is best for them. One example of this subservience to professionalism is that many parents feel they are merely lay participants in the rearing of their own children. This dichotomy between the providers and the recipients of services has led to some serious definitional issues when policy makers have attempted to reach for grass-roots involvement both in the development of policy and in the design of programs to carry out that policy. Grass-roots involvement seldom extends down to the neighborhood organizations (mediating structures). A few cases in point: In August 1979, under the President's Reorganization Project, plans were made to help local communities make better use of available federal and private funds to provide services to teenagers with a history of drug abuse and unemployment. One of the key private agencies that would be implementing this new program is the 4-H Council. The White House Conference on the Family boasted of its success in reaching out to such grass-roots organizations as the Duchess County Long Island branch of the American Association of University Women and the County Family Service Society. This is not to impugn the motives or intent of these very worthwhile organizations, but they can hardly be said to encompass a broad cross section of the country's population.

These definitional issues were taken into account in the mediating structures policy framework. It consists of the following guidelines for both the development of new public policies and the evaluation of existing policies:

- Those close to or experiencing the problem to be addressed should play a primary role in its solution.
- The needs of the child should be satisfied first within the context of the family, either nuclear or extended, and within the culture in which that child resides.
- If existing neighborhood facilities are unable to provide the services needed, every effort should be made to develop such a resource by educating and training indigenous people and institutional representatives, with professional providers of services supplying technical assistance in a spirit of voluntarism.

- When the nature of the problem is such that outside professional assistance can respond effectively, service should be provided in such a way that those being helped will participate fully in the decision making.
- The goal of all assistance should be to strengthen existing social and kinship ties, social conventions, and cooperative networks to enable these associations to develop the capacity to address the immediate and long-range needs of the community. Physical facilities, information systems, and evaluative techniques should be geared toward building the capacity of neighborhoods to replace a street culture of violence and mayhem with the positive culture of community.

With these policy guidelines in mind, the following policy recommendations are offered.

JUVENILE DELINQUENCY PREVENTION

Research

Research should shift its concentration from behavior-centered problems of individual deviant youths and their subculture to an inventory of strengths within populations at risk. The objective should be to assess the successful methods and techniques employed by those who have survived in high-crime communities. More attention should be given to the impact of economic conditions on populations at risk.

- Research on deviant youths should cease to command the bulk of funding committed to the study of juvenile delinquency.
- Representatives of the target populations under study should be encouraged to play a greater role in conducting research.
- The technical skills possessed by professional research institutions should be shared with neighborhood people to enable them to assess the impact of their own activities and make more informed decisions about their own participation in various kinds of research.
- More studies should be devoted to the impact of the fear of crime and its corrosive effect on the behavior of neighborhoods and less attention given to studies of victimization.

- Better methods and techniques must be found to assess neighborhood crime prevention efforts and measure the results quantitatively.
- The effect of neighborhood-based crime prevention programs on the commercial life of the neighborhood should be measured and a closer relationship established between the neighborhood and the business community.
- Identification of subjects to be researched should emanate in part from the sector of the society experiencing the problem to which the study is addressed.
- Studies should be undertaken to determine the sanctions and rewards that effectively do influence behavior within a given cultural environment. All current assumptions in juvenile justice practice about behavioral influences operating for minority juveniles should be critically reexamined.
- Juvenile offenders from poor families, who have been found guilty of a serious offense by the court and sentenced to a restrictive institutional setting, should be afforded the same quality of treatment as the children of more affluent families. The state should provide a voucher to the parents of these youngsters that would enable them to shop for an institutional setting in both the public and the private markets. Viable alternatives must be made available.

Program Policy

- Nuclear and extended families that have successfully raised children in urban areas characterized by a high incidence of crime should be used as principal service providers to youngsters with a penchant for delinquency. Such families could also be used to assist other families in coping with stressful conditions.
- Indigenous institutions serving populations at risk should play a primary role in the delivery of delinquency prevention services.
- The cultural and ethnic traditions that often represent the cornerstone of the social infrastructure of a neighborhood should be incorporated in the design of programs to control and prevent youth crime.
- Policies to deinstitutionalize status offenders or to separate them in restrictive institutions should be distinct from program policies

to control and prevent serious youth crime. Separate legislative categories should be established.

- The number of alternative behavioral options should be increased for youngsters living in populations at risk by reinforcing the stabilizing indigenous institutions in the neighborhoods.
- Policy should move away from support of large-scale criminal justice bureaucracies as the primary agent of reform and service delivery because of the perverse financial incentives to maintain caseloads as a condition of fund support.[4]

Programs should be based on an analysis of policies that have worked, as opposed to some presumed cause-and-effect relation. Program initiatives should be derived from empirical studies of neighborhood-based approaches to the control and prevention of crime that appear to be effective. Common elements that are identified should form the basis for major initiatives and should be shared with other indigenous neighborhood organizations and groups.

CHILD WELFARE AND FAMILY POLICIES

The fields of juvenile justice and child welfare are still considered the "tinker toys" of reformers. It is believed by many that child welfare reformers should be exempt from challenge because they presume to be acting in the best interest of the child. Many such reformers populate the child welfare bureaucracies. Now our challenge is to develop the means to save the children from their champions. As someone once remarked, "God, save me from those who help me in Your name."

Entrenched bureaucratic interests portend far more disastrous consequences for the welfare of youth in populations at risk than any law-and-order backlash emanating from legislative halls or judicial chambers. As pointed out earlier in this book, when restrictive laws are imposed to control and prevent crime, they are seldom effective, as in the case of the New York drug laws and the District of Columbia preventive detention. But the Rockefeller drug law could at least be held up to public scrutiny and evaluated on the basis of several indexes, such as the number of arrests and convictions for drug-related offenses and estimates of changes in the amount of drugs being trafficked. Professional and bureaucratic practices, however, are shielded from such direct accounting.

Jerome Miller, former youth commissioner for the Commonwealth of Massachusetts and the person largely responsible for demonstrating that delinquents can be safely cared for in community-based facilities, writes, "If training schools were ever to be reopened, it would not be a result of rightwing backlash, but would rather be due to the actions of professionals often associated with the liberal community coming in and professionalizing the institutional arrangements." He further contends, "One can find the appropriate psychiatrist, psychologist, social worker, or chaplain to stand out front and bless the most inhumane of human treatment."[5]

It is difficult to draw sharp distinctions between the policies that affect dependent and neglected youngsters and those labeled delinquent. Many of the policies intended to aid needy children instead contribute to their delinquency. There should also be clear distinctions between activities intended to deinstitutionalize and separate status offenders and policies intended to control and prevent youth crime. Legislative and other recommendations for child welfare and family policies are:

- A major goal should be the removal of financial incentives to take children from their natural homes and place them in various institutional settings. The federal government should establish a timetable with appropriate sunset provisions to scale down federal funds going to the states for foster care.
- When it is necessary to remove a child from his home, he should be placed when possible within the neighborhood or within the extended kinship group, otherwise, an indigenous organization should be empowered to seek placement within the community and culture in which the child resides.
- Parents of children in need of out-of-home placement should be given a voucher that would enable them to shop for services (such as foster homes or group homes) in both the public and the private sectors.
- There should be a review of the definitions of "dependent" and "neglected" and the standards by which families are judged worthy of caring for a child, as foster parents, adoptive parents, or as someone offering temporary shelter. Often such decisions

are made in a cultural vacuum, according to a single set of standards without respect for cultural pluralism and diversity.

- Studies should be undertaken to determine the range of definitions of "dependency" and "neglect" and "parental suitability" within various cultures throughout the country.

- More resources should be provided cultural and ethnic groups to help them establish their own methods and techniques for assisting neglected children. Knowledge of the various standards applied in different cultures should be disseminated so that more intelligent decisions can be made in the establishment of general standards of child care.

- The concentration of children's programs into specialized categories of professionalized service delivery systems is antithetical to the interest of mediating structures; therefore, policies should move away from greater specialization to an integration of services at the lowest administrative level.

- Each state should be required by law to maintain accurate records of the children in placement both inside and outside the state, so that the scope of the problem can be properly ascertained. There should be a review of rules, regulations, and practices that act as disincentives for families to remain together. The cultural and ethnic background of the recipients of child care services should be a key factor in assessing their need and determining appropriate action. Permanent homes should be found for those youngsters that are defined as hard to place; they are usually older and tend to be from minority groups. Minority groups and organizations should be permitted to play a dominant role in determining acceptable placement standards and should be provided with the resources to place the child in the extended family networks. No category of people should be denied an opportunity to care for a youngster because of race, ethnic background, income, or class.

- The requirements for state certification of placement homes and facilities should be revised to reflect the cultural diversity of the children most in need of permanent homes. An inventory should be undertaken of the strengths of the communities from which hard-to-place children come, and placement standards should reflect such empirical information.

- The recommendations contained in *Children without Homes*, a report published by the Children's Defense Fund, should be given careful consideration because they would help to strengthen the American family.[6]

URBAN POLICY RECOMMENDATIONS

If the preceding policy recommendations were fully implemented so that local mediating structures, such as the House of Umoja, were able to broaden their influence over the lives of the youngsters they serve, the survival of these programs would still not be guaranteed. Their well-being is also dependent on the economic life of the community. John McKnight and his colleagues at Northwestern University addressed this point: "The social and political institutions may be the heart and soul of a community, but these economic resources supply the essential blood. Income represents the basic plasma while capital and credit act like the iron, without which the whole body becomes anemic and loses its resistance to disease."[7]

Several programs that have successfully improved the overall climate of the community find themselves the potential victims of their own success. The Center for Community Change, a nonprofit community service organization in Washington, D.C., that also serves as an advocate for grass-roots groups elsewhere, reports that several of its constituents are becoming concerned about gentrification and displacement in their neighborhoods. Improvements they have made are now attracting middle-income people and pushing out many of the poor. Speculation is also increasing: "Gentrification is likely to increase. Energy cost, an increase in the formation of small households, and increasing reinvestment in the inner-city will strengthen this trend. This will increase displacement of lower income people unless new policies are developed to ensure that they benefit rather than suffer from the 'back to the city' movement."[8]

At present, those who determine the fate of this country's neighborhoods and who are responsible for the major decisions regarding the economic life of a community seldom seek the opinions of the residents who will be most affected. The same set of negative assumptions that adversely affects the design and implementation of juvenile justice and child welfare policies also pervades the treatment afforded neighborhood people by both public and private economic decision makers. A small but increasing number of people throughout the nation, however, are actively exploring the issues surrounding the economic development of neighborhoods. Strategies are being designed to enhance the survival of local communities, making them more self-reliant economically and less dependent on government. These new advocates are drawn from different disciplines, ideological persuasions, and political affiliations.

The recommendations contained in this section represent a summary of the "state of the art," a cross section of recent conferences, planning documents, and research papers addressing neighborhood investment strategies. Special acknowledgment is given to the Center for Urban Affairs at Northwestern University, directed by John McKnight and his colleague Stanley Hallett, and to others whose work gives fresh insight into the problems and possibilities of strengthening the capacity of neighborhoods by capitalizing on their strengths.

Few, if any, people can state unequivocally that any particular strategy will be effective in bringing about a rebirth of urban centers. I have encountered no one who is prepared to offer a "new" system to replace the present public and private mechanisms that control the economic life in this country. What can be said is that the existing system of conducting business, if allowed to continue, will certainly bring about the demise of neighborhoods as we know them. Old assumptions must be challenged, traditional wisdom must be questioned, and new approaches must be evolved with regard to the causes of urban decline.

The mediating structures and the people they serve must be the primary beneficiaries of the fruits of their own labor as their needs and interest compete with demands of interests outside their control. The points of strategic balance must be understood within the framework of the economic life of the neighborhood, the region, and the nation as a whole. The relationship of the neighborhood to the development process is described by John McKnight and his colleagues:

> Without an understanding of the structures and functions of neighborhood institutions and their relationship to the components of the neighborhood economy, neighborhood development policy has little substance or direction. . . . no public policy can attempt to define exactly what institutions and structures ought to exist in a neighborhood or what the neighborhood economy should be. What public policy can do is attempt to consider the sets of relationships and processes which must exist to involve the residents, the government, the private business sector and the financial and investment institu-

tions in an ongoing participation in the development and maintenance of the neighborhood.[9]

The following recommendations are intended to identify some of the essential ingredients and guidelines for policy development:

- The principal aim of public policy should be to strengthen the capacity of economic institutions within neighborhoods, and to identify and support activities that will create wealth within the communities as well as increase the resilience and diversity of the economies. Programs should be designed to produce the fullest employment of the resources of the neighborhood, including its people, its indigenous capital, and its land.

- A principal policy objective should be to increase the number of firms that are created or expanded within a neighborhood. An inventory of existing neighborhood enterprises should be made to determine which ones demonstrate unique and promising features. A market survey should ascertain the consumer products and services that characterize the neighborhood.

- In accordance with the minimalist proposition of the mediating structures paradigm, under no circumstances should public policy directly involve larger bureaucratic institutions in the establishment of a local mediating structure. Nor should public policy intervene directly in the operation of a local structure or otherwise exercise control over its decision-making process. Any program of economic aid should not depend on subsidy for its long-term continuation.

- It is necessary to identify and assess the needs of a neighborhood as perceived and interpreted by residents directly experiencing the problems associated with urban decline, as opposed to the current reliance upon census data or other special macrostudies.

- Risk taking should be encouraged on the part of neighborhood residents, and public policy that discourages risk taking should be avoided. In addition to maintaining a floor under the incomes of the poor residents, public policy should aim to transform maintenance dollars into development dollars whenever possible.

- Public policy should be based on an accurate understanding of the true costs of and returns to local activities—not simply the internal returns and costs of development ventures.

- Various strategies of income transfer investment should be supported as a means of increasing the amount of money available for investment in existing neighborhoods.

- Government incentives for job creation should be directed to small, independent businesses and enterprises, which are the largest generators of new jobs in the American economy. The corollary to this is a deemphasis on tax incentives for large corporations to relocate within urban areas characterized by high unemployment.
- Programs to motivate and train young people for work should use local mediating structures as the principal vehicle for offering such services.
- Building codes, zoning restrictions, and other regulatory mechanisms should be carefully reviewed to determine whether they represent a legitimate protection of public interest or whether such codes and statutes protect only special interests.[10]
- Every effort should be extended to institute programs that better redistribute existing resources and avoid increasing public expenditures that contribute to inflation.

REFERENCES

1. Donald and Rachel Warren, "Helping Networks: How People Cope with Problems in the Metropolitan Community, Final Report," Monograph Project 3-ROI-MH-2498, National Institute of Mental Health, December 31, 1976.

2. Arthur Naperstek, "Neighborhood and Family Service," unpublished paper, Research Project, University of Southern California, Washington Campus, June 1979.

3. Peter L. Berger and Richard John Neuhaus, *To Empower People* (Washington: American Enterprise Institute, 1977).

4. Examples of abuse abound. In New York City the Transit Police received $500,000 to divert delinquent youngsters from the criminal justice system. When the supply of youngsters eligible for diversion dried up, however, officers were encouraged to round up youthful offenders for minor infractions and charge them with delinquency so that the unit could continue to receive federal funds. To increase their incentives for arrest, the police officers were told that the "diversion" would be equated with a felony arrest on personnel evaluation reports. (*New York Daily News,* September 4, 1979).

5. Jerome Miller, "The Serious Juvenile Offender," a paper prepared for the

Symposium on Juvenile Offenders sponsored by the School of Criminal Justice, State University of New York, Albany, October 1977.

6. *Children without Homes* (Washington, D.C.: Children's Defense Fund, April 1977).

7. John McKnight et al., "Community Development Policy Paper: Structural Disinvestment, A Problem in Search of a Policy," unpublished manuscript, Center for Urban Affairs, Northwestern University, 1979, p. 4.

8. Center for Community Change, "Report to the Board of Directors," July 25, 1979.

9. McKnight et al., "Community Development," p. 27.

10. Many states, for example, restrict the use of plastic pipe in the construction and rehabilitation of houses, even though it is one-third as expensive and just as durable as lead pipe. Any increase in the cost adversely affects the price of housing to the poor.

INDEX

141

New Deal, 111
Newsweek, 117
"No knock" law, 16

Office of Economic Opportunity, 19-20, 93
Office of Juvenile Justice and Delinquency
Prevention, 2, 3-4, 7-8
Ohlin, Lloyd, 20
Omnibus Crime Control and Safe Streets
Act (1968), 15
Organization of time and space, personal,
77-78

Parole, 23-24
Peer group, 34, 70, 77, 107
counseling, 100, 102
Philadelphia, Pennsylvania, 45, 50, 53, 60-
63, 65, 66, 79-80
Philadelphia Council of Black Clergy, 52-53
Policy. *See* Juvenile justice policy; Eco-
nomic policy; Urban policy
President's Reorganization Project, 129
Preventive detention, 16, 132
Primary bonds, 33, 36, 40, 89, 105
importance in rehabilitation, 34-35, 37,
42, 89-90, 97-99, 100, 102, 107
Probation, 6, 23-24
Professional-client relations, 24, 72, 106
Professionals, 17, 19, 20-22, 38, 129. *See
also* Bureaucracies and bureaucratic
practices.
Provo experiment, 28
Psychotherapy. *See* Mental health strategies
Public concern about juvenile crime, 1, 15
Punishment. *See* Crime control strategies;
Deterrence strategy; Incarceration
at the House of Umoja, 51-52

Race and the delinquent population, 4, 8-
10, 12-13
Rainwater, Lee, 115, 116
Recidivism, 4, 6-7, 12, 28, 43. *See also*
Chronic offenders
Release programs, 23-24
Report of the National Advisory Commis-
sion on Civil Disorders, 117-118
Research
on efficacy of crime control strategies, 2,
5-13, 28, 89
methodological problems of, 6, 7
priorities for, 130-131
Resources, allocation of, 10, 122
Retribution, 15
Rockefeller drug law, 16, 132
Rockmore, Tyrone "Flash," 69

Role modeling, 23, 24, 25, 28, 49
Role playing, 48

Scale, 120
Scanzoni, John H., 41
Segregation of delinquent population, 3-4,
7-8, 12-13, 28
Selby, Robert, 77-78
Self-sufficiency, 123-124
Service. *See* Community based programs
Smith, Michael E., 3
Social and economic conditions, common to
members of community based programs,
68, 102, 103, 105
See also Criminogenic environment
Social change strategies, 19-21
Socioeconomic status of young offenders, 8,
9-10, 12-13
South Arsenal Neighborhood Development
Program (SAND), 90, 102-105
SAND Everywhere School, 104
SAND Home Orientation Program, 104-105
Strengths of Black Families, The (Hill), 42
Sudarkasa, Niara, 41
Sun Oil, 100
Surrogate Family. *See* Community based
programs
Svirdoff, Michael, 114-115

To Empower People (Berger and Neuhaus),
128

Umoja, House of, 45-88, 102, 135
and community service, 55-56, 78-81,
86-87
family structure of, 42-43, 50, 68-70, 71
funding of, 52-53, 58-60, 82-86
and mediation in gang disputes, 60-62, 72,
76
relations with public institutions, 53-54,
57-60, 61, 82-86
Umoja, principles of, 51, 73
U.S. Department of Housing and Urban
Development, 104
U.S. Department of Justice, 2, 37
Urban Coalition, 52
Urban life, 10-12, 99
Urban policy, 111-112, 127-139. *See also*
Great Society programs
Urban problems, 113, 118

Values, 25, 26-27, 36, 39, 106
in community based programs, 40, 81, 93,
97-98, 107

ABOUT THE AUTHOR

Robert Woodson is currently a Resident Fellow at the American Enterprise Institute for Public Policy Research (AEI), where he continues to address the problems of youth crime. He has recently begun a three-year research project on revitilization, aimed at determining what mix of public policies and neighborhood strategies is most likely to produce successful community development. While at AEI, he has served on the President's Commission on Mental Health and on the Task Force on Community Resources; he also participated in the President's reorganization of the Law Enforcement Assistance Administration and was a consultant to the Subcommittee on Crime of the Juvenile Justice Program. Prior to coming to the Institute, Mr. Woodson directed the National Urban League's Administration of Justice Division. He has directed a number of national and local community development programs that include work among a broad cross section of the American public, from blacks in Chicago to farmworkers in California. He has lectured in colleges and universities both in the United States and Europe and has appeared on numerous television talk shows. His publications include "The Challenge of Black Power" (*Trends Magazine*), "Mediating Structures Can Control Youth Crime" (*Taxing and Spending*), and numerous articles in newspapers across the country.